Convenience Stores and Retail Fuel Properties: Essential Appraisal Issues

Readers of this text may also be interested in the following publications from the Appraisal Institute:

- *The Appraisal of Real Estate,* 12th Edition
- *A Business Enterprise Value Anthology*
- *The Dictionary of Real Estate Appraisal,* 4th Edition
- *Valuing Contaminated Properties: An Appraisal Institute Anthology*

Convenience Stores and Retail Fuel Properties: Essential Appraisal Issues

by Robert E. Bainbridge, MAI, SRA

Appraisal Institute · 550 W. Van Buren · Chicago, Illinois 60607 · www.appraisalinstitute.org

Reviewers:	Stephen A. Manning, MAI, SRA
	Michael S. MaRous, MAI, SRA
	John A. Schwartz, MAI
Vice President, Educational Programs and Publications:	Larisa Phillips
Director, Publications:	Stephanie Shea-Joyce
Editor:	Mary Elizabeth Geraci
Supervisor, Book Design/Production:	Michael Landis
Production Specialist:	Lynne Mattick-Payne

For Educational Purposes Only

The material presented in this text has been reviewed by members of the Appraisal Institute, but the opinions and procedures set forth by the author are not necessarily endorsed as the only methodology consistent with proper appraisal practice. While a great deal of care has been taken to provide accurate and current information, neither the Appraisal Institute nor its editors and staff assume responsibility for the accuracy of the data contained herein. Further, the general principles and conclusions presented in this text are subject to local, state, and federal laws and regulations, court cases, and any revisions of the same. This publication is sold for educational purposes with the understanding that the publisher is not engaged in rendering legal, accounting, or other professional service.

Nondiscrimination Policy

The Appraisal Institute advocates equal opportunity and nondiscrimination in the appraisal profession and conducts its activities in accordance with applicable federal, state, and local laws.

Printed in the United States of America

Library of Congress Cataloging-in-Publication Data

Bainbridge, Robert E.
    Convenience stores and retail fuel properties : essential appraisal issues / by Robert E. Bainbridge
       p. cm.
    ISBN 0-922154-76-7
        1. Real property–Valuation. 2. Convenience stores–Valuation. 3. Service stations–Valuation. I. Title.

HD1387.B3636 2003
658.8'7–dc21

               2003050259

Table of Contents

Foreword

Convenience Stores and Retail Fuel Properties: Essential Appraisal Issues is an indispensable resource that can help appraisers, lenders, investors, and operators of convenience stores and retail fuel properties understand how the design and operation of these unique retail properties contribute to their income and value.

This book addresses important physical and functional changes in modern convenience stores and describes the innovative steps convenience store operators take to survive in the face of new and growing competition. In addition to extensive information on industry trends and terminology, the text provides instructions for investigating the supply of and demand for convenience stores in local markets and demonstrates the application of the three approaches to value.

Convenience Stores and Retail Fuel Properties: Essential Appraisal Issues contains details about convenience stores and petroleum-marketing properties that cannot be found in any other text. It will be valuable to those who regularly value convenience stores and need to keep up with the rapid changes taking place in the industry as well as those who may be asked to appraise a convenience store or retail fuel property in the future.

Alan E. Hummel, SRA
2003 President
Appraisal Institute

About the Author

Robert E. Bainbridge MAI, SRA, is Director of Property Tax Services for C-Store Valuations, a firm that specializes in providing expert witness testimony on litigation and valuation issues to the convenience store industry. He is a member of the International Association of Assessing Officers and the National Association of Convenience Stores. Bainbridge holds a BBA in real estate with specialized studies in regional and urban economics and has taught college courses in real estate appraising. He is a past contributor to the *The Appraisal Journal.*

Introduction

Convenience Stores and Retail Fuel Properties: Essential Appraisal Issues is expressly designed to augment the experienced appraiser's general knowledge and skill. It provides instruction in the appraisal of convenience stores and petroleum-marketing properties, but it does not present material about basic appraisal theories or fundamental appraisal practices.

It is impossible for an appraiser to conduct a productive interview with the convenience store owner, buyer, or seller without a working knowledge of the industry. When discussing a convenience store appraisal with an owner-operator, the appraiser must realize that fuel margins are less than in-store margins, that a new store's average cost exceeds $1 million, and that the owner-operator struggles to compete with hypermarkets and mass merchandisers.

Convenience Stores and Retail Fuel Properties: Essential Appraisal Issues is structured like an appraisal report. Chapter 1 begins with a discussion of techniques used to assess and analyze convenience stores. Chapter 2 analyzes the supply of and demand for convenience stores in the subject's local market. Chapter 3 describes site assessment. Chapter 4 assists the appraiser in analyzing and describing store design and construction. Chapter 5 familiarizes the appraiser with fuel service, which includes fuel dispensers, underground storage tanks, and canopies. Chapter 6 discusses non-real estate components classified as furniture, fixtures, and equipment, and Chapter 7 explores specific valuation issues appraisers encounter in the appraisal of convenience stores and petroleum-marketing properties.

Chapters 1 through 6 are designed to educate the appraiser about the industry and current convenience store business trends. They also provide the convenience store appraiser with a working vocabulary. The valuation process can be considered only when the appraiser fully understands the economic and operational nature of convenience stores.

Chapter 7 provides an in-depth discussion of how the cost, sales comparison, and income capitalization approaches apply to convenience stores. The systematic and comprehensive analysis of the industry and local market presented in the previous chapters is equally useful for appraising proposed stores and existing properties. The current state of the industry, the economic conditions of the local trade area, and the adequacy of the site and improvements will ultimately determine how the appraiser estimates store profitability. This judgment is important to making the income allocation in the income capitalization approach.

Convenience Stores and Retail Fuel Properties: Essential Appraisal Issues is the most comprehensive work available about the appraisal of convenience stores and petroleum-marketing properties. With the continued expansion of the Internet, information is easier to obtain than ever before. Nearly everyone has access to information about any subject, including the convenience store industry, and given the amount of detailed information that is now available to appraisers, they are required to know more about the properties they value than in the past. If convenience store fuel sales trends for the last 20 years are available from convenience store industry trade associations on the Internet and the convenience store appraiser does not acquire that information, the appraiser will seem incompetent and irresponsible.

Ultimately, the abundance of online information could transform real estate appraisers from generalists to specialists. Appraisers will become experts in specific property types because vast amounts of industry, demographic, and technical information about various property types are readily available. In the future, appraisers will know much about little, instead of little about much. Let's begin by discussing the convenience store industry in Chapter 1.

Robert E. Bainbridge, MAI, SRA
Ontario, Oregon

Chapter

1

Total Sale

Industry Assessment

What Is a Convenience Store?

The question "What is a convenience store?" is not an easy one to answer. For the last several years the National Association of Convenience Stores (NACS), an industry trade association, has defined a convenience store as:

> a retail business with primary emphasis placed on providing the public a convenient location to quickly purchase from a wide array of consumable products (predominantly food or food and gasoline) and services. While such operating features are not a required condition of membership, convenience stores have the following characteristics:
>
> - While building size may vary significantly, typically the size will be less than 5,000 square feet.
> - Off-street parking and/or convenient pedestrian access.
> - Extended hours of operation with many open 24 hours, seven days a week.
> - Convenience stores stock at least 500 stock keeping units (SKUs).
> - Product mix includes grocery-type items, and also includes items from the following groups: beverages, snacks (including confections) and tobacco.[1]

Some convenience stores are small—less than 500 square feet, while others, at 7,000 square feet, are the size of a neighborhood grocery store. Many convenience

1. National Association of Convenience Stores, "What Is a Convenience Store?" *2001 Convenience Store Industry Fact Book* (Alexandria, Va.: National Association of Convenience Stores, 2001).

stores offer co-branded fast food and the stores of tomorrow may include pharmacies or banking services.

Today's market is characterized by the blurring of retail channels, with a wide variety of retail concepts and overlapping competition. For example, the recent 2-in-1 concept pairs a full-size fast food restaurant such as A&W with a traditional fuel marketer such as Chevron. Wal-Mart, Costco, and other mass merchandisers are selling their own brands of motor fuel for the first time ever. Jack-in-the-Box Inc. is beginning to test market a convenience store and retail fuel concept that it will build alongside the new hamburger restaurants it opens. Traditional convenience store operators view Walgreens, Rite Aid, and similar new neighborhood drug retailers as "convenience stores for women" because of their competing merchandise lines that are targeted toward female customers.

History of the Convenience Store Industry

The following information about the convenience store's origin is taken from the article "History of the Convenience Store Industry," which can be found on Brown & Williamson's Web site.

> According to the National Association of Convenience Stores, "convenience stores evolved from a variety of sources early in the twentieth century." They drew upon characteristics of many types of retail establishments in existence at the time: the "mom-and-pop" neighborhood grocery store, the "ice-house" (from pre-refrigerator days), the dairy store, the supermarket and the delicatessen.
>
> The Southland Ice Company is credited with the birth of the convenience store in May 1927 on the corner of 12th and Edgefield Streets in the Oak Cliff section of Dallas, Texas. "Uncle Johnny" Jefferson Green, who ran the Southland Ice Dock in Oak Cliff, realized that customers sometimes needed to buy things such as bread, milk and eggs after the local grocery stores were closed. Unlike the local grocery stores, his store was already open 16 hours a day, seven days a week; so, he decided to stock a few of those staple items. The idea turned out to be very convenient for customers.
>
> By the end of World War II, automobiles became more prominent and sparked the rapid growth of the convenience store industry. According to NACS, "The automobile helped fuel the growth of suburban living—of families wanting the "American Dream." Americans, with bigger cars and better roads, began flocking to the suburbs where they found plenty of space to live and raise children... but too much space between shopping centers."
>
> The industry grew rapidly along with this consumer need for convenient shopping and supplanted the neighborhood grocery stores and became established in new suburbs and areas too small to warrant a supermarket. Once again, convenience store companies were opportunistic and innovative, thriving in market niches too small for others to operate profitably.
>
> Today, the main competitors convenience stores face are those mentioned above as well as chain drug stores, superettes, warehouse stores, general retail stores, home delivery services and, of course, other convenience stores.[2]

2. Brown & Williamson Tobacco Co., "History of the Convenience Store Industry" (Brown & Williamson Tobacco Co., 2003).

The Convenience Retailing Industry

The NACS, one of the largest convenience store industry trade organizations in the country, offers this historical sketch of the convenience store retailing industry:

In the not too distant past, every convenience store looked about the same—2,400 square feet of packaged consumer items. Today, companies in the industry are approaching their markets with different types of stores and different product offerings. There are mini-convenience stores under canopies, conventional size stores with expanded foodservice, and even hyper-convenience stores with an extensive variety of product offerings and in-store seating for foodservice.

The fastest growing segments of the convenience store market are considered by many to be "non-traditional" stores. That is, store formats other than 2,400 square feet, either larger or smaller.

The changes in store formats have implications for all elements of the industry. Retailing executives are concerned with competitive impact and their marketing strategies and niches. Product suppliers need to be aware of format variations as they dictate requirements for appropriate product packaging, promotion and distribution for the stores. Equipment and systems vendors have to design their equipment and systems to fit the various types of store formats. Investors and financial analysts must understand the economics of the changes taking place and the likely impact on the convenience store industry. Local, state and federal governmental agencies also want to understand the various store formats.

Based on this research, six formats were identified as representing trends in the convenience store industry. The six convenience store formats are:

- Kiosk
- Mini convenience store
- Limited selection convenience store
- Traditional convenience store
- Expanded convenience store
- Hyper convenience store

A general description of each type is provided below.

Kiosk

This format is less than 800 square feet and is intended to provide some additional revenue beyond gasoline sales. Gasoline is always the focus of this operation with the owner usually being an oil company or petroleum marketer. These stores sell only the fast-moving items found in traditional convenience stores (tobacco, beverages, snacks, and confections). Grocery items are conspicuously absent, as is any sort of foodservice. Store sales may be only about ten percent of revenues in such locations. Parking is usually only at the pumps. Hours vary widely depending on the location and the inclinations of the owner. Typical customers are transients and locals stopping in to buy gasoline.

Mini Convenience Store

This store format, usually 800 to 1,200 square feet in size is extremely popular with oil companies and the emphasis is on gasoline sales. However, in such locations, the owners view store sales as an important part of the revenue and margin picture. Grocery selection is usually very thin and foodservice beyond prepared sandwiches is rare. There usually is not any parking other than that at the pumps, although some locations do have modest striped parking. These stores are open from 18 to 24 hours a day. Customers are usually people buying gasoline. However, there are stores of this size in urban areas that may or may not sell gasoline.

Limited Selection Convenience Store

These stores, which range from 1,500 to 2,200 square feet, are becoming more numerous. They are often affiliated with oil companies and are in the size range of a converted two-bay service station. Both gasoline and store sales are generally important parts of profitability. They differ from the "mini convenience store" in a broader product mix and grocery offering (although still somewhat limited by traditional convenience store standards). Also, simple foodservice (hot dogs, nachos, popcorn, etc.) may be offered. Although gasoline buyers are normally still the main part of the customer base, traditional convenience store patrons are important. Striped parking and extended hours are common.

Traditional Convenience Store

Most of the original convenience stores fall into this category. They are about 2,400 to 2,500 square feet in size and offer a product mix which includes dairy, bakery, snack foods, beverages, tobacco, grocery, health and beauty aids, confections, and perhaps, prepared foods to go, fresh or frozen meats, gasoline, various services, and limited produce items. Most stores of this size have 6 to 12 striped parking spaces or some form of convenient pedestrian access. Hours are extended compared to average retailers with a large percentage open 24 hours per day. Such operations are normally owned by convenience store chains, but oil companies have also built or acquired stores of this size.

Expanded Convenience Store

Growth is occurring in the number of stores in the 2,800 to 3,600 square feet range. Such stores can accommodate more shelving for additional grocery products or room for significant fast food operations and seating. Stores using the space for more grocery items are taking advantage of the niche that has developed as supermarkets increasingly move above the 40,000 square foot range. A few large chains are using this "superette" approach. A greater percentage is using the space to take advantage of the high profit margins in fast foods. As the number of smaller operations proliferates (largely as a result of the oil companies), many convenience store chains apparently view the move towards increased fast foods as essential. In terms of other products and services, such stores usually carry the traditional convenience store items. Parking is important with most having about 10 to 20 marked spaces. Hours are extended. Such operations not only attract the typical convenience store customer but also more families, women, and senior citizens.

Hyper Convenience Store

These very large stores (4,000 to 5,000 square feet) usually offer an array of products and services arranged in departments. For example, such stores may offer variations such as a bakery, a sit-down restaurant area, or a pharmacy. Many of these locations sell gasoline.The number of employees per shift can be large, particularly if a small restaurant is present.

The number of parking spaces is substantial, especially since the amount of time the average customer spends in such an establishment can be significant. Hours are extended. Here again, as in the case of the expanded convenience store, families and senior citizens as well as traditional convenience store customers are patrons. In some locations, such stores are mini-truck stops that obviously affect product mix and the customer base.[3]

Trends in Store Growth

The economic growth Americans enjoyed throughout the 1990s came to an abrupt halt in 1999, when industry growth leveled off. In response to the slowing economy, the number of new convenience stores being built dropped by 3.1%. Faced with competition from other retail channels and smaller margins, 1.1% of convenience stores closed. The decline continued, and in 2000 the number of convenience store closings increased to 2%.

Trends in Industry Fuel, Merchandise Sales, Food Service, and Profits

After nearly 10 years of uninterrupted growth in gross sales and profits, the convenience store industry is changing again, but not due to growth. Per-store profits were down 4.1% in 2001 from the previous year. The primary causes of the decline are lower fuel volumes and lower margins. Stores have experienced lower fuel volumes due to higher retail prices and competition from other retail competitors such as hypermarkets and supermarkets, which have begun selling fuel. Both fuel and in-store sales have experienced lower profit margins due to higher fuel and cigarette prices and increased competition from drugstores and restaurants.

Appraisers should be cautious when examining retail sales levels from year to year. In 1999, for example, the Consumer Price Index (CPI) for cigarettes jumped 31% as a result of price increases implemented in 1998 and 1999 by tobacco manufacturers in response to the Master Settlement Agreement. In 2000, the CPI for gasoline jumped 28.5%. This time it was the result of crude oil price spikes and refining and distribution problems. Because tobacco and gasoline are two of the largest product categories for convenience stores, these price increases can severely impact the gross revenue of convenience stores. That does not translate into increased profits for convenience store operators, however. In fact, a convenience store operator's profits often decline in periods of rapid retail price increases. Operators, fearful of losing market share in a highly competitive industry, are reluctant to pass price increases at the wholesale level on to their retail customers. Typically, only part of a wholesale price increase is passed on at one time. The convenience store operator tries to absorb some of the increase over the short term and in so doing reduces store profits.

3. *Convenience Store Industry Marketing Strategies and Store Formats*, National Association of Convenience Stores research report, 2001.

The convenience store industry divides store sales into five broad categories. The appraiser should determine the trend in the subject store's performance in these areas over the previous three years and compare it to industry averages. The five categories are

1. Motor fuel sales
2. In-store sales
3. Merchandise sales
4. Services
5. Food service

Motor Fuel Sales

Gasoline and diesel fuel are considered separately, but both are included in this category. The gasoline distribution system in the United States is massive. Moving gasoline to approximately 200,000 retail outlets throughout the United States has required the development of a complex distribution infrastructure. The complexity of the market structure is reflected in the multiple pricing levels (classes of trade) for gasoline. Thus, before it reaches the consumer, gasoline may be sold in one or more wholesale transactions.

• Gasoline is sold by refiners as it leaves the refinery at so-called "refinery gate" prices.

• Gasoline is sold by refiners or by resellers as it leaves a distribution terminal at so-called "rack" prices. ("Rack" refers to the superstructure of pipes, hoses, and manifolds that delivers the product into a tank truck or tank wagon.)

• Gasoline is sold by refiners or resellers to retailers at the gasoline service station at so-called "dealer tank wagon" prices.

Both refinery gate prices and rack prices are influenced primarily by spot or futures prices or both. At a minimum, rack prices will conceptually exceed refinery gate prices by the cost to transport the gasoline from the refinery to the terminal, usually by pipeline or barge.

Dealer tank wagon prices represent the cost of the product to the gasoline retailer. In addition to reflecting overall market conditions, dealer tank wagon prices include payments for additional services that a supplier may provide to a retailer, especially a "branded" retailer–a gasoline station that sells gasoline under the name of a large oil company.

The services a supplier provides to a branded retailer may include trademark use, credit card service, advertising, and security of supply. Security of supply means that when supplies are short, a nationally branded store can receive gasoline from an oil company refinery before an independent operator does.

Gasoline retail marketing follows a variety of structures and contractual arrangements. Some convenience stores, for instance, are owned by a refiner. Most, however, are owned by an independent operator. The cost structure of convenience stores also varies, as may the convenience store's marketing stance, and hence, its margin.

Pre-tax gasoline retail prices are set by retailers such as convenience store operators. The price on the gas pump reflects pre-tax gasoline retail prices plus taxes. Pre-tax prices reflect both the retailer's purchase cost for the product and other costs of operating the convenience store. Pre-tax prices also reflect local market conditions and factors such as the desirability of the location and the operator's marketing stance.

Although fluctuating retail prices make it difficult to pinpoint exact figures, motor fuel sales currently comprise about 61% of the industry's total sales. In 1995, the ratio of motor fuel sales to in-store sales was about 50:50. As a result, today's convenience store industry is highly dependent on fuel sales revenue. Approximately one-half of the revenue of a typical convenience store will come from fuel sales and the other half from in-store sales.

Some stores are weighted more toward fuel sales, while others have more in-store sales. Appraisers should determine a store's motor fuel sales by examining the store's operating statements for the last three years. It is essential to know the number of gallons of gasoline sold each year, rather than the retail sales levels for those years. For example, the number of gallons sold each year could decline, while a 30% price hike in the retail price per gallon would make the financial statements appear as though fuel sales were increasing.

The number of fuel gallons sold each year is, in effect, a proxy or measure of the overall quality of operations. A convenience store situated in a poor location will sell little fuel, while a convenience store in a good location will sell a great deal of fuel. An older, outdated store design with older mechanical pumps will sell less fuel than will a modern facility, all other factors being equal. A convenience store surrounded by numerous competitors may experience reduced fuel sales, so it is important that an appraiser carefully consider the number of gallons the subject store has sold annually in the last three years and compare that number to industry averages for the same time period.

During an interview, the appraiser should ask the convenience store operator what factors have affected fuel sales for that store during the past three years. Road construction, new competition, and wholesale price volatility all can distort any given year's gallonage. For the convenience store appraiser, the number of gallons sold each year is one of the most important numbers to obtain and understand.

To help appraisers better understand the convenience store owner-operator's fuel sales business, they should be aware that domestic gasoline consumption has increased by 39% in the last 20 years and, since 1980, the number of registered vehicles has risen from 162 million to 213 million. Mileage per vehicle also increased in that period–from 9,400 miles annually to more than 12,200 miles. Tables 1.1 and 1.2 show additional data that can help appraisers further understand a convenience store operator's standing in the fuel sales business.

As Table 1.1 indicates, 87% of the cost of a gallon of gasoline is fixed before it arrives at the convenience store. After the costs of crude oil; federal, state, and local taxes; and refining and margin costs have been deducted, only 13% of the cost remains for the convenience store operator. This is called the *gross fuel margin*. The gross fuel margin is the difference between what the wholesaler charges for a gallon of gasoline and the retail price that the convenience store owner-operator can obtain in the local market.

Table
1.1	**Factors That Impact Gasoline Prices**

Cost Factor	Percentage of Retail Price
Cost of crude oil	42
Federal, state, and local taxes	29
Refining and margin costs	16
All other distribution and marketing costs	13

Source: National Association of Convenience Stores, "Gasoline Prices Fact Sheet."

From this 13% gross margin, convenience store operators pay all of their associated costs, such as credit card fees (usually 2%–4%), wages for attendants and cashiers, utilities and advertising costs, taxes, repairs, and maintenance fees. Whatever income remains after all of these expenses have been paid constitutes the net profit before income taxes.

The gross margin on fuel has consistently been approximately $0.13 per gallon since 1996. However, as Table 1.2 shows, the gross margin as a percentage of sales varies widely as the retail price of gasoline fluctuates.

Table
1.2	**Fuel Margins**

	Cents per Gallon	Percent of Sales
1996	13.1	10.7
1997	13.4	11.3
1998	12.6	12.0
1999	13.4	11.7
2000	13.3	9.3

Source: National Association of Convenience Stores.

Convenience store fuel sales today include unleaded, blend, and premium grades of gasoline and diesel, and their gross margins can vary. However, the industry usually describes the average fuel margin for a particular store rather than attempting to track the different margins on all four fuel products. The convenience store industry sometimes calls this average fuel margin the *pool margin.*

In-Store Sales

In-store sales generally include revenue that is not fuel-related nor produced as a result of a carwash business. Appraisers should remember that in-store sales include merchandise, food service, and services and will account for about 40% to 50% of the typical convenience store's revenue.

The average convenience store will carry about 2,870 stock keeping units, or SKUs. SKUs are the total number of products available for sale that are in the store's inventory at any given time. For example, a package of cigarettes, if sold as a package, is one SKU. A carton of cigarettes, if sold as a carton, also is one SKU. The top four in-store categories are: cigarettes, 36%; food service, 13%; packaged, non-alcohol beverages, 12%; and beer, 12%. Combined, the products in these categories account for nearly three-quarters of all in-store sales.

As discussed under motor fuel sales, an appraiser should be cautious in analyzing the subject store's sales trends when major product categories are experiencing volatile price fluctuations. For example, in 2000 two major price increases were instituted by cigarette manufacturers. A $1.30 per carton increase occurred in January, followed by a $0.60 per carton increase in July. These increases were not market driven, but resulted from the Master Settlement Agreement negotiated between 46 states and the leading cigarette manufacturers. An increase such as this one at the wholesale level can distort the sales trend for the store being appraised. In this case, what would appear to be an 11% increase in cigarette sales actually would be a 4% decline in real terms when the sales figures are deflated by the wholesale price increases.

Such distortions illustrate why it is important to examine margin dollars from year to year and not just trends in gross revenue. Cigarette consumption is actually declining in the United States and the convenience store industry needs to recognize the danger of being dependent on the success of its cigarette sales.

Food Service

Food service refers to fresh food prepared onsite. It does not pertain to pre-packaged items for retail sale. Food service revenue may be significant, as with a co-branded restaurant, or it may be modest in stores that have only a few linear feet of counter space devoted to fresh food items. A nationally branded *quick service restaurant (QSR)* can double the total revenue for a location, allowing convenience store operators to select higher priced real estate than would be possible with a stand-alone unit. Incremental sales typically increase by as much as 20%. For a time, branded QSRs experimented with smaller express units within convenience stores that typically had limited menus. Many of these units failed to perform according to convenience store industry expectations. Today, most national chains prefer to build full-service restaurants attached to convenience stores, with full trade dress and exterior signage. The more recent concept of a full-service restaurant joined to a full-size convenience store is called a *2 in 1*.

The *average unit volume (AUV)* for a QSR chain located within a convenience store is a primary tool restaurants use to gauge performance and potential profitability. The average unit volume depends on the size of the QSR, the size of the average check, and whether the unit is located off a highway or in a residential area.

Average unit volumes for branded QSRs vary widely. The hamburger category posts the highest AUV, at $658,000. That figure is skewed upward because of the $950,000 average of Jack-In-The-Box and the $900,000 average of McDonald's restaurants. The Mexican food category has the lowest average volumes, averaging $200,000. Its low average volumes are likely the result of the smaller kiosks and limited-size units in Mexican food service. Snack AUVs also are relatively low at $220,000.

A performance measure closely related to the AUV is the *annual sales per square foot*. The annual sales per square foot is the average unit volume divided by the square footage of the operation. The annual sales per square foot typically is used in the industry to compare restaurant units within the same menu segment. The chicken category reported the highest sales per square foot ($484) in 2000. Among national QSRs, Dunkin' Donuts posted the highest sales per square foot at $1,000, and White Castle reported average sales per square foot of $922.

A *franchise fee* is an upfront fee charged to operators by the franchisor to license a concept. National QSR chains charge the highest franchise fees, and burger chain franchise fees are among the highest. Burger King charges $37,500 for a franchise fee, and Wendy's charges $25,000. At the other end of the spectrum, Subway's franchise fee is comparatively low at $10,000, and Domino's is even lower at $3,250. The franchise fee is not paid every year, so it does not play a role in a food service's annual operations. However, the franchise fee does factor into the costs of building a new convenience store with branded food service.

Royalties and *advertising fees* are ongoing payments to the franchisor to cover administrative and marketing costs. They are usually based on a percentage of gross or net sales. Most national QSR chains collect royalties ranging from 4% to 8%, and typical advertising fees range from 3% to 4%. Sometimes the advertising fees are built into the cost of the branded products that the franchisees are required to purchase.

Furniture, fixtures, and equipment (FF&E) includes the cost of outfitting a food service unit with seating, grills, and point-of-service (POS) systems. These costs can vary widely depending on the concept and building type. A Pizza Inn requiring only dedicated space, for example, requires just $6,000 in FF&E. Burger King and snack concepts, however, have the highest FF&E costs, ranging from $227,000 for a Carl's Jr. to $235,000 for a Dairy Queen. Often specialized equipment such as grills and soft-serve ice cream machines is required. The gross margins for licensing of franchised fast food had been approximately 60% for most of the 1995-1999 period; in 2000 margins in this category declined to 53%. The NACS 2002 *State of the Industry Report* concludes:

> Branded QSR chains play a significant role in convenience store food service, and their presence is expected to continue to grow. Several concepts are expected to gain the most penetration in the near future, based on planned openings. The most aggressive of these are Chester Fried Chicken, which expects to open 600 units, and Subway, which is planning 100 openings. McDonald's expansion plans call for 75 additional units in 2001.

Profits

The median pre-tax profit per store in 2000 was $25,403, or 1.7% of gross sales. This is a 13% decline from the $29,206 level in 1999.

Services

As profits from fuel sales decline, the services category, which includes copy machines, ATM revenue, and money orders, may become a more important category in coming years. Even now, convenience stores are beginning to offer auto service (oil and lube) and dry-cleaning services.

Blurring of Distinction Among Retail Channels

Retail gasoline sites at hypermarket locations grew by 66 sites per month in the early part of 2001. As of September 2001, 1,596 hypermarkets in the United States, such as Wal-Mart and Costco, had retail gasoline sites. The average hypermarket continues to add six sites per month, and retail gasoline sites are increasing across the nation. Some industry analysts even predict that 5,360 hypermarkets will sell 22.8 billion gallons of gasoline and capture 16% of the U.S. gasoline market by 2005. The following article, "Blurring of Distinction Among Retail Channels," characterizes the most important issue facing the convenience store industry today–the entrance of hypermarkets and supermarkets into the gasoline retailing business.[4]

> There's a serious brawl taking place these days at the pumps and parking lots of retail America. While no injuries have been reported, casualties are expected. As well as opportunities.
>
> Welcome to the new world of gasoline retailing, where traditional operators are being threatened into submission by mega-billion-dollar heavyweights like Costco, Wal-

4. VNU Business Media, Inc. *Convenience Store News* (New York: VNU Business Media Inc., 2002).

Mart, Ahold USA and other prominent high-volume merchants planting fuel islands on their lots.

Fuel Census—a cross-channel survey and analysis conducted by Convenience Store News and distributed to sister publications Retail Technology, Retail Merchandiser and Progressive Grocer—explores this rapidly changing market, delving into the unique characteristics each channel brings to the retail petroleum segment.

While consumption remains largely stagnant, high-volume corporate titans see gasoline as a profitable pipeline, bringing motorists into their stores, and from the stores to the pump. For them, gasoline is a natural extension toward "one-stop" shopping. The motives behind these operators' interest in gasoline differ, however.

For mass merchants, gasoline means value-added service, a "thank you." For supermarkets, it's a cross-merchandising vehicle—get in-store coupons at the pump, receive gas credits at the checkout. For shopping clubs, cheap gas is often one more reason for members to renew and newcomers to entertain membership. And for traditional fuel operators, the changing scene marks a clarion call to enhance customer services and embrace new technology.

For product manufacturers, the arrival of high-volume retailers means unrivaled technological advances from sleek payment systems and marketing/loyalty solutions to enhanced underground monitoring and fuel inventory devices. For retailers, the changing landscape means new opportunities and risks.

What Fuel Census says more than anything else is "The times, they are a-changin'," that today's obscure player could be tomorrow's gasoline destination, and that today's retail hotshots who rest on their laurels could be tomorrow's casualties.

A New Mirastar Fuel Center at Wal-Mart

For hypermarkets such as Wal-Mart and its Mirastar fuel centers, the addition of on-site fueling allows additional sales on the property. However, since these hypermarkets do not need to acquire more land to sell motor fuels, the investment may be viewed as marginal. Many of these hypermarket sites sell more than 250,000 gallons of gasoline per month, compared to the average convenience store, which sells roughly 105,000 gallons per month.

Sources of Data

National Association of Convenience Stores (NACS)
www.nacsonline.com.
1600 Duke Street, Alexandria, VA 22314 (703) 684-3600

State of the Industry Report, published annually. Exhaustive amount of data on industry totals, trends, and averages.

VNU Business Media Inc.
Convenience Store News
www.csnews.com
770 Broadway, New York, NY 10003 (646) 654-4500
Comprehensive and useful data on store operations and profit margins.

Petroleum Marketing Institute
www.pmaa.org
Current issues for petroleum-marketing facilities and trends in the oil industry.

Local Supply and Demand Assessment

More convenience stores have been being constructed in the United States every year since 1994. Figure 2.1 shows the trend in the number of convenience stores nationwide from 1990 to 2000. Table 2.1 details how many stores opened and closed each year during the same period.

Figure

2.1 **Store Count**

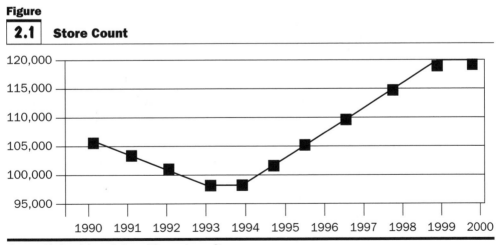

Source: National Association of Convenience Stores

Table

2.1 | National Convenience Store Supply Trends from 1990–2000

Year	(%)	New Stores Opened Number	(%)	Stores Acquired Number	(%)	Total Increase Number	(%)	Stores Sold or Closed Number	(%)	Net Increase Number	Total Number
2000	N/A*	N/A*	N/A*	N/A*	N/A*	N/A*	N/A*	N/A*	N/A*	400	119,800
1999	N/A*	N/A*	N/A*	N/A*	N/A*	N/A*	N/A*	N/A*	N/A*	5,700	119,400
1998	5.02	5,707	2.53	2,871	7.54	8,578	-4.21	(4,785)	3	4,900	113,700
1997	4.59	4,992	2.86	3,109	7.45	8,101	-4.24	(4,616)	160	4,200	108,800
1996	4.64	4,857	3.30	3,448	7.94	8,305	-4.72	(4,940)	110	3,500	104,600
1995	1.56	1,575	3.32	3,355	4.88	4,930	-5.25	(5,312)	0	2,900	101,100
1994	1.16	1,141	1.33	1,307	2.49	2,448	-3.14	(3,082)	-20	(200)	98,200
1993	1.25	1,230	0.97	957	2.22	2,187	-4.57	(4,498)	-240	(2,400)	98,400
1992	1.41	1,419	2.05	2,062	3.45	3,481	-5.85	(5,892)	-250	(2,600)	100,800
1991	4.04	4,175	2.53	2,613	6.56	6,788	-6.22	(6,432)	-230	(2,400)	103,400
1990	3.91	4,137	4.40	4,658	8.31	8,795	-6.93	(7,333)	140	1,500	105,800

Source: National Association of Convenience Stores

Convenience store supply is generally thought of as the number of stores within any given market. Appraisers should know that as the number of convenience stores has increased in the last nine years, so has stores' average floor space. Today, the average convenience store is 2,407 square feet; new stores currently being built, however, average 3,413 square feet.

Regional Growth

According to a C-Store.com survey completed in 2002, the western United States experienced the fastest growth in the number of convenience stores that year. Combined with information from the 2000 census, the results of the C-Store.com analysis indicate that the population of the United States is moving West. "It is no surprise the West enjoys both the greatest population growth since 1995 (9.7%) and the fastest c-store growth (44.3%)," the study stated. Nationally, there is an estimated customer base of 2,372 per convenience store; in the West, that figure is substantially larger, with 2,913 people per store. The West will continue to be the fastest growing market for c-stores over the next five years, according to C-Store.com.

Table 2.2 shows the number of convenience stores in each of the 50 states, along with each state's percentage of the national total. Note that Texas, California, and Florida have the most convenience stores.

Table

| 2.2 | 2001 Convenience Store Count by State |

State	Stores	%	State	Stores	%
Alabama	2,783	2.32	Montana	469	0.39
Alaska	133	0.11	Nebraska	849	0.71
Arizona	1,919	1.60	Nevada	776	0.65
Arkansas	1,568	1.31	New Hampshire	719	0.60
California	9,482	7.92	New Jersey	1,851	1.55
Colorado	1,786	1.49	New Mexico	862	0.72
Connecticut	1,218	1.02	New York	4,752	3.97
Delaware	273	0.23	North Carolina	4,892	4.09
Dist. of Columbia	173	0.14	North Dakota	298	0.25
Florida	7,876	6.58	Ohio	4,565	3.81
Georgia	4,677	3.91	Oklahoma	2,287	1.91
Hawaii	331	0.28	Oregon	1,422	1.19
Idaho	693	0.58	Pennsylvania	3,866	3.23
Illinois	3,848	3.21	Rhode Island	347	0.29
Indiana	2,451	2.05	South Carolina	2,792	2.33
Iowa	1,674	1.40	South Dakota	390	0.33
Kansas	1,177	0.98	Tennessee	2,939	2.45
Kentucky	2,241	1.87	Texas	12,331	10.30
Louisiana	2,642	2.21	Utah	893	0.75
Maine	939	0.78	Vermont	501	0.42
Maryland	1,409	1.18	Virginia	3,223	2.69
Massachusetts	2,328	1.94	Washington	2,632	2.20
Michigan	3,952	3.30	West Virginia	1,259	1.05
Minnesota	2,101	1.75	Wisconsin	2,139	1.79
Mississippi	1,882	1.57	Wyoming	296	0.25
Missouri	2,845	2.38	Total	119,751	100.00

Source: National Association of Convenience Stores.

Trade Area Analysis Tools

A *trade area* is the geographical area within which the subject convenience store competes for business. The trade area for a typical convenience store is considered by the industry to have a two-mile radius in urban areas. Alternately, in small rural communities the trade area often covers a major portion of the town or even an entire city. For convenience stores located adjacent to freeways or highways, the trade area may cover several miles along a particular traffic route.

Consider a proposed rural store located on a highway that is the only north-south route in that part of the state. The highway parallels a river and for several miles runs along the bottom of a canyon. There are no alternate routes or intersecting highways for several miles. In this case, the trade area could conceivably extend 30 miles in each direction from the subject convenience store.

Trade area analysis most often involves either ring studies or slightly more sophisticated drive-time studies, diagrams of which are shown in Figures 2.2 and 2.3. *Ring studies* simply identify geographic areas described as circles with particular radii measured from the subject property. Typically one-, three-, and five-mile rings around the subject store are plotted on a map.

Drive-time studies are similar to ring studies except they take into consideration accessibility to the subject over the existing traffic routes. Physical barriers such as rivers, mountains, and railroad tracks are factors in drive-time studies. Three-, five- and seven-minute driving times to the subject are estimated along various traffic routes.

Trade area studies attempt to assemble all of the pertinent demographic information within a designated trade area. Demographic data, which includes population count, median age, disposable income levels, ethnicity, and other population characteristics, identifies the factors affecting the demand for any given convenience store. Many proprietary firms supply demographic information, which is typically based on U.S. census data.

Appraisal Institute members can access LoopNet's "Any Site Demographics" feature online and in minutes have a demographic printout with detailed breakouts for population, number of households, race and ethnicity, income, age, and median housing values. A printable map with customized ring settings is also included. This service is free to subscribers.

Supply is measured by the number of competitive properties within a particular trade area. Property profiles of all competitive properties within a trade

Figure

2.2 | **Ring Study**

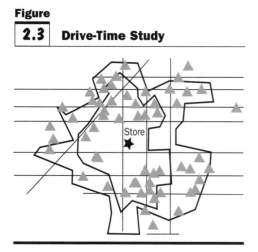

Figure

2.3 | **Drive-Time Study**

area are arranged by a trade area analyst. The typical features noted in property profiles are

- Store size
- Parking
- Visibility
- External appearance/age
- Overall pricing (high, average, low)
- Fuel branding
- Fuel service (canopy, dispensers, point-of-sale readers)
- Food service
- Weekly hours of operation
- Services (ATM, public restrooms)

The convenience store appraiser should include separate descriptive profiles of each competitive property within the subject's trade area. A photograph of each competitive property also is helpful. Using a form greatly facilitates recording data in the field and has the added benefit of ensuring that all pertinent data is included. An example of a competitive property profile is shown in Table 2.3.

It should be noted that the fuel pricing information gathered on the competitive properties will be useful to the appraiser when processing the income capitalization approach later in the appraisal. The market price per gallon for the various grades of fuel will be correlated to estimate the subject's fuel sales revenue on the reconstructed operating statement.

Proprietary firms that perform trade area analysis typically apply some type of statistical modeling to the supply and demand information previously discussed to make a projection of the subject store's fuel sales and in-store sales. A market niche may be identified or the trade area could be considered saturated.

How a numerical measure of supply and demand is determined from the field data is the trade secret of the firm selling the service. Oil companies construct econometric models to estimate fuel demand at a potential retail location, but these models are not normally shared with third parties. For proposed construction appraisal assignments, the appraiser should ask fuel wholesalers what their projections of the subject property's gallonage are. The appraiser will then consider the information when completing revenue projections for the subject.

Beyond gathering the data and making general interpretations, any modeling function is beyond the scope of this discussion and the services most appraisers provide. Alternatives to statistical modeling include the location quotient analysis and the service station saturation index (SSSI), a trade area analysis tool developed by Texaco. These trade area analysis tools are simple and easy to construct.

Table

2.3   Sample Field Data Collection Form

Competitive Profile

General		Store Facility	
Name	Walt's Texaco	Store size	3,600 sq. ft.
Address	196 U.S. Highway 95	Site size	200 ft. x 100 ft.
City, State	Riggins, Idaho	Parking	20
Store brand	Texaco	Forecourt	Adequate
Fuel brand	Texaco	Age	2 yrs.
Weekly hours	168	Design	Good
Location		Refrigerator doors	14
Primary road	U.S. highway	Shelf islands	6
Traffic count	4,000 ADT	Scanners	Yes
Visibility	Good	Restrooms	Yes/ADA
Frontage	200 feet	ATM	Yes
Curb cuts	Two	Alcohol sales	Yes
Corner location	Yes	Carwash	Roll-over
Fuel Service		**Food Service**	
Canopy size	24 ft. x 80 ft.	Type	QSR
Fueling positions	8	Branded	A&W
Lighting	Good	Breakfast/lunch/dinner	Lunch/dinner
Dispensers	(6) 3-hose MPD	Drive-thru	Yes
Pay-at -pump	Yes	Inside seats	20
Price/gallon regular	$1.499	**Ratings**	
Price/gallon blend	$1.599	Overall	Good
Price/gallon premium	$1.699	Cleanliness	Excellent
Price of diesel	$1.399	Dairy case	Excellent
Credit cards	Yes	Product display	Excellent
		Parking/circulation	Average

Comments: Site is too small for semi-trucks.

Location Quotient Analysis[1]

How does an appraiser analyze the local market, and how can an appraiser determine if the local market for the subject is oversupplied or undersupplied? One tool that can help answer these questions is the *location quotient*, a measure of the tendency of a particular type of business or industry to locate in a geographic area. A simple calculation widely used in various regional economic applications, the

1.   Robert E. Bainbridge, MAI, SRA, "Analyzing the Market for Convenience Stores" *The Appraisal Journal,* (October 2000).

location quotient is well suited to analyzing the local convenience store market. The concept also is easy for readers of appraisal reports to understand. To calculate the particular location quotient, an appraiser will need the following information: the population of the local market area (Xa); the number of convenience stores operating in the market area (Ya); the population for the benchmark region (Xb); and the number of convenience stores in the overall region (Yb). These four factors are described below.

1. The population of the market area (Xa). In smaller cities and towns, it is often appropriate to define the market as the entire community. The market could be a neighborhood or a segment of a larger metropolitan area. Regardless, the population of the local market area is one of the simplest numbers to obtain. Local government agencies, the U.S. Department of the Census, and local universities usually have the necessary population figures.

2. The number of convenience stores operating in the market area (Ya). If the market area is a small, rural community, the appraiser may simply count the convenience stores and use the Yellow Pages listings for convenience stores as a reference. These listings also can be found on the Internet, and many Web sites will plot them on a map. If the subject is a freeway location, the market area may extend several miles along the traffic corridor. The appraiser should aim to isolate all businesses selling gasoline that are potential competitors.

3. The population for the benchmark region (Xb). The overall region is most easily defined as the state where the subject is located. This figure will be used only as a distribution benchmark; it does not contribute to defining the market area. Typically the appraiser can proceed on the assumption that the distribution of convenience stores throughout the state is a normal market distribution. The location quotient analysis will indicate whether the local market has more or fewer people per store than the region being used as a benchmark. State population figures are readily available, and state agencies such as the Department of Commerce typically have the necessary figures.

4. The number of convenience stores in the overall region (Yb). The best source for this number is the National Association of Convenience Stores, an industry association that publishes a state-by-state count each year. The association's Web address is *www.nacsonline.com*. For similar state-by-state counts and store growth projections for each state, see *www.c-store.com*. This information is free and no registration is required.

Appraisers should be certain to match the year of the population count to the year of the published store count. It is unlikely that the store distribution for the state will change much from one year to the next, so there is little danger in using a population figure and store count from two years ago.

Appraisers should strive to find the numerical relationship between the population and the number of stores. The number of stores does not have to be for the current year. It usually takes at least a year before store counts are compiled and published by the industry.

Typically, the location quotient derived will be a number greater than or less than one. If the number is less than one, e.g., 0.55, the subject market's population is insufficient to support the existing number of convenience stores, at least as compared to the base region distribution.

In this example, the population is only 55% of the total needed and would have to nearly double before the number of persons per store would be comparable to the region as a whole. Alternately, if the number is greater than one, the local market has more people per store than the base region and new store development would be appealing. Finally, if the location quotient is exactly one, the local market matches the regional distribution of stores to population.

The location quotient is useful for quantifying supply and demand in the local market. However, appraisers should be circumspect in applying the results. Other factors that play an important role in the results of the calculation include

- Proximity to traffic corridors such as major highways
- A higher percentage of travelers (as opposed to local customers) who may patronize the subject
- An unusual traffic count

In other words, the conclusions of a location quotient study should be judiciously applied.

With a national population of 281,421,906 in 2000, the ratio of population to convenience stores was 2,350:1. The location quotient for convenience stores simply measures the relationship between the number of local convenience stores and the population of the local market compared to the relationship for some base region. The base region may be a county, several counties, or an entire state. The location quotient is determined using the following calculation:

$$(Xa/Xb) \div (Ya/Yb)$$

where

Xa is the population of area a

Xb is the population of area b

Ya is the store count of area a

Yb is the store count of area b

and assume a is the local market and b is the base region.

Another useful supply and demand analysis tool is the service station saturation index.

Service Station Saturation Index

Each convenience store must share the total volume of gasoline used by the automobiles with other stores in the trade area. Although this trade area analysis tool was developed by Texaco[2] in the 1960s for service stations, the concept is still useful for analyzing the local convenience store market.

The service station saturation index (SSSI) expresses the number of convenience stores in a trade area as a percentage of the number required to provide adequate service at a profit. A balanced market will have an SSSI of 100. If the SSSI is 200, then there are twice as many stores as can be supported.

Texaco did not provide any norms or standards to set up a formula. However, the formula can be constructed as follows:

$$[ANS/[(C \times GPC)/GPSR]] \times 100$$

where:

ANS = The actual number of stores in the trade area

C = The number of cars in the trade area

GPC = The number of gallons consumed per car per year

GPSR = The gallons per store required for profitable operation

If there were 10,000 cars in the trade area and each car consumed 700 gallons of gasoline per year, the gross gasoline volume would be 7 million gallons per year. If it takes 600,000 gallons per year for a store to be profitable, then the trade area would support approximately 12 convenience stores. If there are 24 stores selling fuel in the trade area, the SSSI would equal 200.

The SSSI is useful for quantifying the supply and demand of a trade area, but it is important for appraisers to remember that each existing store is given equal weight. That is seldom realistic in any geographic market because fuel volume varies from store to store. The blurring of retail channels is making the SSSI less useful today. However, in certain instances it may help appraisers grapple with challenging supply and demand considerations.

Retail Fuel Information for Local Markets

In smaller markets and trade areas, the convenience store appraiser usually can develop retail fuel pricing information by inspecting and observing convenience stores in the area. In a larger market, third-party sources can be great assets in compiling competitive pricing information on retail fuel outlets.

One of the most reliable third-party sources is the Oil Price Information Service (OPIS). Its Web site is *www.opisnet.com.* The site shows averages for daily,

---

2.   The concept of the SSSI was published in the *Encyclopedia of Real Estate Appraising,* 3rd ed. (Englewood Cliffs: Prentice-Hall, 1978), 957.

weekly, and monthly fuel prices in 360 major metropolitan markets, including prices for all grades of gasoline and diesel. A sample of an OPIS retail price report is shown in Table 2.4. Individual fuel outlets are identified.

As mentioned in Chapter 1, the rack price is the wholesaler's cost of fuel. The "rack" refers to the distribution superstructure at the pipeline terminal. OPIS publishes the "rack-to-retail" margins for key U.S. regions. These margin reports also compare profitability across zip codes and track three-year averages. OPIS is the single most important source of information that convenience store operators use to compare fuel margins in specific markets.

Another useful site is *www.gaspricewatch.com*. This is the Web site of a consumer advocacy group. Individual retail fuel outlets are searchable by zip code. News articles relating to the retail gasoline market also are available on this site.

Table

2.4 Sample Retail Price Report From OPIS

Sample State Report for Rhode Island

This sample shows only a portion of the stations for the state of RI

Station ID	Company	Address	St	City	Brand	Date	Reg	Mid	Pre
95001678	Sunoco Srvc Station	206 Broad St	RI	Ashaway	Sunoco	12/5/00	163.9	171.9	178.9
83064573	Db Mart #25	216 Main St	RI	Ashaway	Citgo	12/5/00	162.9	170.9	177.9
30007318	Barrington Getty	227 County Rd	RI	Barrington	Getty	12/5/00	161.9	169.9	176.9
88004862	Saunders Bros., Inc.	242 County Rd/ waseca	RI	Barrington	Shell	12/5/00	161.9	169.9	176.9
88004864	J. Enterprises, Inc	579 Metacom Ave.	RI	Bristol	Shell	15/5/00	169.9	177.9	179.9
88026150	Bristol Shell	412 Metacom Av/hopwt	RI	Bristol	Shell	12/5/00	168.9	176.9	183.9
30005571	Bristol Getty	1282 Hope St	RI	Bristol	Getty	12/5/00	168.9	176.9	183.9
95007855	Sunoco Srvc Station	1064 Hope St	RI	Bristol	Sunoco	12/5/00	168.9	176.9	183.9
98003189	Cumberland Farms, Inc	400 Metacom Ave.	RI	Bristol	Gulf	12/5/00	167.9	175.9	182.9
20006719	Sprague EnergyCorp	5680 Post Rd	RI	Charlestown	Texaco	12/5/00	163.9	171.9	178.9
98002565	Cumberland Farm/Gulf	4169 Old Post Rd	RI	Charlestown	Gulf	12/5/00	163.9	173.9	180.9
20009235	I Chahine & N Kiriak	Putman Pike & Victor	RI	Chepachet	Texaco	12/5/00	171.9	179.9	186.9

Source: Oil Price Information Service

Ring Studies–Any Site Demographics
http://appraiser.loop.net.com
This is part of the Appraisal Institute's LoopNet and requires an annual subscription. After logging in, go to "Appraiser Tools" and select "Any Site Demographics." Users will be prompted to enter a street address or map coordinates and see a local map displayed. Users of this site can custom size the radius of the rings and instantly obtain a demographic printout of the population count, age characteristics, racial composition, income levels, and number of housing units within those rings.

Traffic Counts
The transportation departments of each state maintain a variety of data on traffic volume. Municipalities sometimes commission private firms to complete traffic studies, so the appraiser should ask the city clerk, engineering department, or planning department if any studies have recently been done.

Traffic engineering firms can estimate the number of visits a proposed convenience store will receive based on traffic patterns at a particular location. However, traffic count studies can be costly.

Retail Fuel Prices and Margins
www.opisnet.com
Oil Price Information Service (OPIS)
This service covers all major U.S. markets and tracks retail and wholesale prices on all grades of fuel. It also provides margin reports and is a good source of pricing and margins for motor fuel.

Gas Price Watch
www.gaspricewatch.com
This site has retail fuel locations searchable by zip code.

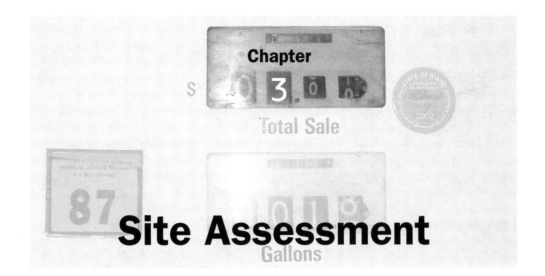

Chapter

3

Site Assessment

In valuing a convenience store site, appraisers must consider the site from the perspective of its retail earnings potential. In other words, how well suited is the site to generating retail sales? All convenience stores require good visibility, easy access, and heavy traffic. Even the simplest property and store characteristics play an important role in a convenience store's value. This chapter explores the requirements convenience store owners and operators should consider to ensure a store's success and the details appraisers should note when assigning value to convenience store properties.

A convenience store site consists of three functional components: access, the forecourt, and the store envelope. A description of each follows.

Access

Easy access to a site is an absolute necessity if a convenience store is to thrive. All other factors being equal, the site with the most convenient access will attract the most customers. For a convenience store in an urban setting, the industry considers 100 feet of frontage to be the minimum amount of space necessary for access. For a location with truck fueling, a minimum of 300 feet of frontage and adequate space for vehicles to turn around are essential.

Forecourt

The *forecourt* is the area where fuel dispensers and canopies are located. It typically is located between the street and the store.

Store Envelope

The *store envelope* includes the building footprint, the drive-thru lane, and parking. Many local zoning ordinances are drafted from model legislation and call for a minimum of 3.3 on-site parking spaces for every 1,000 square feet of building area.

Location Criteria

Appraisers should understand what a convenience store developer looks for in a potential site. Site selection criteria vary from company to company, depending on the company's target market and business model. The following summary of location criteria for convenience food stores was prepared by the Planning and Development Department of Surrey, British Columbia, and highlights points appraisers should consider when assessing a convenience store site.

Location Criteria for Convenience Food Stores

Primary market area. Clusters of grocery stores indicate that many local grocery stores are sharing the one-mile radius trade area used by convenience store chains. Thus, the actual trade area is about a 1/2-mile radius.

Vehicle traffic count. Approximately 80% of convenience stores are located on major collector roads, which carry 2,000 to 15,000 cars per day.

Traffic speed limit. Ninety percent of convenience stores were located along roads with traffic speed limits of 30 mph to 45 mph. Traffic speeds should be high enough to be convenient, but low enough to permit safe access.

"Going-home" side of the street. The preferred location is on the side of the road where the afternoon traffic volume is heaviest so that many customers see the convenience store before reaching their homes.

Convenience store competition. In general, chain convenience stores ignore the presence of independent stores. With a wider product mix, chain stores have a larger market area or more intense market penetration than the independents. Chains carry little or no produce or meats, so they consider themselves to be in a slightly different market.

Supermarkets and shopping plazas in the trade area. Other retail properties are an advantage because they increase the visibility of the convenience store. A location between the source of customers and the shopping center permits the convenience store to intercept some of the supermarket trade.

A corner site. A corner location is preferred to one in the middle of the block because of increased visibility.

Ease of ingress and egress. Easy ingress and egress makes it convenient and safe to shop at the store. (Stop signs, traffic lights, and raised medians will influence the ease of entry and exit.)

Population density. The greater the number of people within a convenient distance, the higher the sales. Approximately 10,000 people are needed to support one store.

Household density and type. Sales improve when there are large numbers of apartment dwellers between 18 and 35 years of age and households of large families nearby.

Employment and occupation. The major customer groups are white-collar workers (41%) and blue-collar-workers (34%). Housewives, students, and retirees constitute only 25% of customers.

Family income. As an area's median income increases, sales decrease. Areas of middle income are best for sales.

Population mix and age distribution. The main market consists of people aged 18 to 35 years (50%). If retirees are more than 10% of market area population, sales are affected adversely.

Automobile ownership. Two-thirds of the customers arrive by automobile, so the amount of auto ownership in the trade area is important.

Age of houses. Local grocery stores tend to locate in areas that have houses 15 to 35 years old.

Nearby schools. A convenience store should not be located in close proximity to an elementary school.

Hours of operation. The busiest day of the week is Sunday, then Saturday. The busiest time of the day is between 3 p.m. and closing (up to midnight). This period accounts for 62% of daily sales.

Store building characteristics:

- Parking for 10 to 15 cars should be available.
- Store size determines product diversity; older, independent stores have about 800 to 1,000 sq. ft., while convenience chain stores have 2,000 square feet to 2,400 sq. ft.
- Visibility is important. The building and any signs should be clearly visible for at least 700 feet from both sides of the street.

A few additional considerations were offered by the Manitoba Business Service Center in the report *Starting a Convenience Store.* The report states:

Convenience stores offer quick and friendly service, handy locations, a variety of merchandise, and extended hours of operation. This fact sheet focuses on starting an independent convenience store. However, many convenience stores are franchise operations. For example, there are over 7,000 "7-11" franchise convenience stores in North America, Britain, and Japan.

Location

Choosing a location for your store may be your single most important decision. Do your research. In particular, consider these factors:

Population. The Grocery Trade Association states that to sustain a convenience store, between 500 and 1,000 people must live within a one-mile radius of it. If people have to travel more than a mile, they are more likely to go to a supermarket for a major shopping trip. Check an area's future development plans and projected growth rates.

Competition. Although a convenience store's competition is mostly from other convenience stores, it can also come from supermarkets. Study all competitors to see if the local market can support another operation.

Traffic. Impulse purchases make up a large percentage of convenience store sales, so high volumes of pedestrian and vehicle traffic passing a store is critical. Owners/operators should try to locate near schools, parks, sporting facilities, and other businesses (especially in strip malls) to increase traffic. They also should monitor seasonal traffic fluctuations in resort areas and carefully determine whether summer earnings can sustain them during slow, winter months.

Site Costs and the Economics of Co-Branding

Because of the need for good access, visibility, and heavy traffic, convenience stores tend to be developed on expensive sites, and from 1980 to the present costs have increased dramatically. As Table 3.1 and Figure 3.1 show, from 1980 to 2000 the average cost of a convenience store site increased by 694%, an average annual increase of 33%.[1] Between 1990 and 2000, the average cost of a convenience store site increased by 135%, an average annual increase of 12%, and costs continue to climb. The average cost of a convenience store site today is $259,000 in rural areas and $699,800 in urban areas, or $5.86 per square foot in rural areas and $15.80 per square foot in urban areas.

Table 3.1 Cost Trends for Convenience Store Sites

Year	Average Cost	Year	Average Cost
2000	$699,800	1989	$375,300
1999	$530,500	1988	$350,500
1998	$546,400	1987	$266,000
1997	$391,100	1986	$274,400
1996	$425,500	1985	$212,800
1995	$326,400	1984	$170,200
1994	$449,100	1983	$147,900
1993	$447,200	1982	$133,400
1992	$357,100	1981	$89,900
1991	$294,000	1980	$88,100
1990	$298,300		

1. The percentage increases cited here are not compounded.

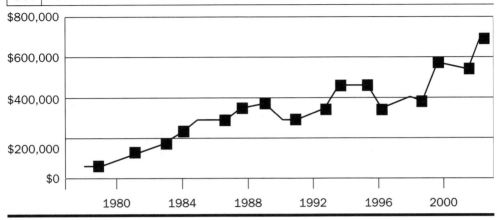

| 3.1 | Cost Trends for Convenience Store Sites |

Source: National Association of Convenience Stores

In the past five years, urban land prices for convenience stores have increased more than rural land prices. Consequently, co-branding a convenience store with a fast food restaurant has become more popular. For example, McDonald's USA claims that shared land can lower development and construction costs. Initial investment savings can range from $150,000 to $250,000, with annual operating savings of $10,000 to $25,000. McDonald's co-branding site criteria for urban and rural locations are shown in Figures 3.2 and 3.3.

McDonald's market criteria for a co-branded facility are no different than the criteria required for a traditional restaurant. The criteria for urban and suburban sites are as listed on the following page.

Figure 3.2

McDonald's Co-Branding Site Criteria for Restaurants in Urban and Suburban Locations

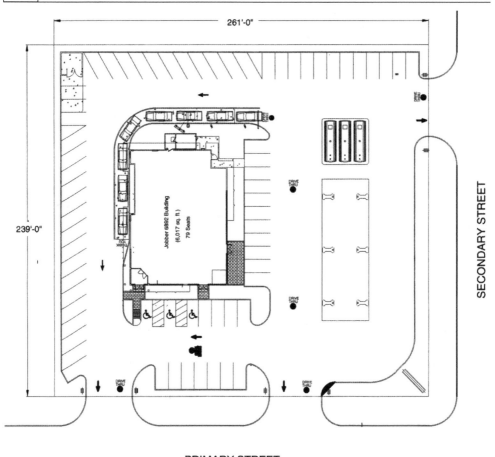

PRIMARY STREET

Source: McDonald's USA Web site

Market Criteria

1. The store should be located in a prime location (i.e., the corner of Main and Main.)

2. The minimum lot size should be approximately 60,000 square feet (depending on setbacks, etc.).

3. Frontage of 250 linear feet is required.

4. Visibility should be excellent.

5. The store should be located near generators such as home, work, and shopping.

6. There should be a total of 65 parking spaces.

7. Total drive-thru stacking should be eight cars.

Figure

3.3 | McDonald's Co-Branding Site Criteria for Restaurants in Rural Locations

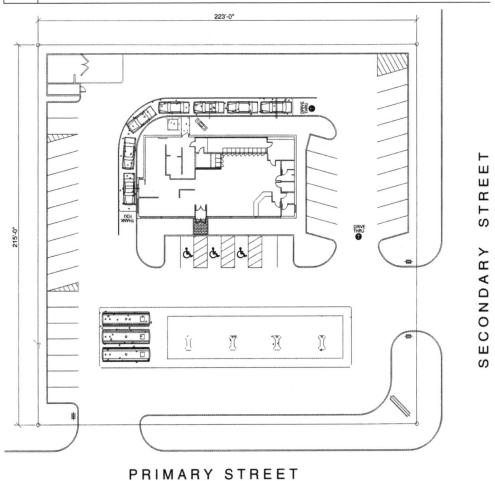

Source: McDonald's USA Website

As previously stated, the market criteria for a McDonald's co-branded restaurant are no different than the criteria required for a traditional restaurant. The criteria for rural sites follow.

Market Criteria

1. The store must be in a prime location (i.e., at the corner of Main and Main.)
2. The approximate lot size should be 48,000 square feet.
3. Frontage should be 223 linear feet.
4. There should be a total of 40 parking spaces.
5. Total drive-thru stacking should be seven cars.

Exxon/Mobil Site Selection Criteria

Not every site is suitable for retail fuel sales, and major oil companies such as Chevron, Shell, and Exxon/Mobil have established minimum criteria that must be met before sites can carry their brands. These site selection criteria are established to help retail operators select sites that will be economically viable. Brand identity and protecting their brand's public image is important to oil companies. When a retail store affiliated with a nationally recognized brand fails, the oil company's image is tainted and the public associates the brand with failure.

A prototype of how oil companies evaluate a potential site, the specific site selection criteria employed by Exxon/Mobil follow.

- Exclusivity of trade area
  A trade area's supply and demand profile is a key factor in site selection.

- High traffic counts
  There should be 20,000 vehicles passing by the convenience store each day.

- +56,000 net usable square feet
  The company will consider less square footage for stores in metro markets.

- Residential density
  There should be 15,000 existing or planned residences within a 1.5-mile radius.

- Excellent visibility
  The site must be visible from one-third of a mile.

- Excellent accessibility
  There should be convenient ingress and egress from both primary and secondary streets.

- Signalized corner intersections
  Ideally, stores should be located at four-corner sites.

- Absence of operating restrictions
  A store can be open 24 hours seven days a week, sell beer and wine, and have a carwash.

The potential for diesel fuel sales is much greater at sites that can accommodate semi trucks than those sites that cannot. However, although a large site may have good semi-truck access and parking space, if the site is situated on a traffic route trucks do not use, it may not be developed for truck fueling.

Due to size and access limitations, not every site allows for semi-truck fueling. To help appraisers set minimum physical requirements for semi-truck access, Exxon/Mobil has design criteria for a site that can accommodate truck fueling (see Figure 3.4).

Figure

3.4 **Exxon/Mobil Site Design**

VERTICAL FOUR ISLAND STARTING GATE - FRONT OF STORE PARKING - FAR CORNER/MID-BLOCK LAYOUT

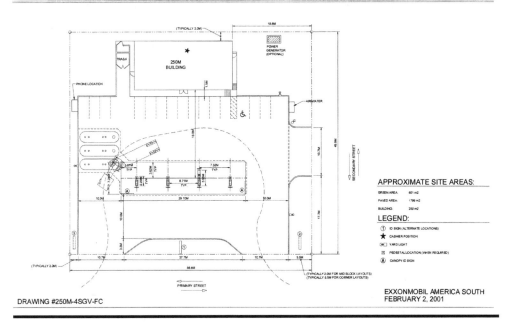

DRAWING #250M-4SGV-FC

EXXONMOBIL AMERICA SOUTH
FEBRUARY 2, 2001

Measuring Traffic Volume and Patterns

As previously stated, traffic volume is one of the most important components convenience store appraisers should consider when valuing a site. Therefore, appraisers should rely on authoritative sources, not owner-operators, for information regarding average daily traffic (ADT) volume.

Detailed, comprehensive information about traffic volume and traffic patterns is available through federal, state, and local government agencies. Table 3.2, taken from the Oregon Department of Transportation's Web site, shows the type of traffic data that these agencies can provide to appraisers. The information is derived from a permanently maintained traffic recording station (ATR) located about one mile from the subject. The appraiser must know where the information was recorded and how well the collected data relates to the subject's location.

Seldom, if ever, would the appraiser attempt to record and collect traffic counts on the job site; it is too time-consuming. As Table 3.2 shows, a location's traffic volume varies from day to day and throughout the year. Peak volume months are easily determined, along with separate columns for weekday versus daily traffic. Note that the daily traffic is higher than the weekday traffic in July, August, and September. More summer tourists and recreational travelers are passing this location on the week-

Table 3.2 Examples of Traffic Data

2000 Harney County ATR Stations

	Weekday Traffic	Percent of ADT	Daily Traffic	Percent of ADT
January	1592	67	1487	63
February	1734	73	1639	69
March	2087	88	2056	87
April	2272	96	2244	95
May	2496	105	2470	104
June	3007	127	2985	126
July	3088	130	3138	132
August	3278	138	3312	140
September	2893	122	2934	124
October	2520	106	2501	106
November	1986	84	1966	83
December	1764	74	1697	72

Vehicle Classification Breakdown	Percent of ADT
Passenger Cars	39.30
Other 2 axle 4 tire vehicles	40.00
Single Unit 2 axle 6 tire	3.80
Single Unit 3 axle	0.50
Single Unit 4 axle or more	0.10
Single Trailer Truck 4 axle or less	4.40
Single Trailer Truck 5 axle	7.40
Single Trailer Truck 6 axle or more	1.50
Dbl-Trailer Truck 5 axle or less	0.00
Dbl-Trailer Truck 6 axle	0.20
Dbl-Trailer 7 axle or more	1.80
Triple Trailer trucks	0.00
Buses	0.50
Motorcycles & Scooters	0.50

Source: Oregon Department of Transportation

end, which accounts for this difference. Table 3.2 also gives a detailed breakdown of the types of vehicles passing this location. The number of passenger cars and a variety of light truck and semi-truck classifications are shown. If the subject is marketing diesel fuel to semi-trucks, this type of vehicle breakdown is important.

Traffic flow analyses show average daily volumes, peak hour and peak day volumes, monthly patterns, turning lane movement at intersections, and vehicle type. Detailed traffic flow analyses are available from state transportation departments at a minimum cost. It is useful for appraisers to collect traffic maps to monitor trends in traffic volumes. With the growth of the Internet, much of this data is now available for free online.

Because convenience store business is affected by the amount of traffic on any given day, it is important for appraisers to understand at what time of year the subject experiences its lowest and highest traffic volumes. Recreational areas can have wide fluctuations in traffic volume, and sometimes the winter traffic volume is not enough to support such an operation financially. For this and other reasons, it is crucial to understand traffic patterns over the course of the year, not just on a daily basis.

The types of vehicles people drive also affect a convenience store's business, particularly stores that market diesel fuel to truck drivers. Information on the average daily traffic volume is not sufficient for an appraiser to value a truck stop convenience store accurately.

Table 3.3, taken from the Oregon Department of Transportation's Web site, is another example of the type of detailed information that state transportation departments provide. This table shows the traffic volumes along particular segments of the highway, allowing the appraiser to determine where the traffic is coming from and where it is going. Table 3.3 also shows the traffic volume changes that occurred during the previous year and the maximum daily and hourly traffic volumes at each counting station.

Traffic engineering firms provide detailed traffic analysis of specific sites as well. For proposed convenience stores, the owner may have already completed these studies as part of loan application requirements. These reports are a tremendous help to appraisers because they can help estimate the subject's potential capture volume based on certain models the traffic engineer employs. Once an appraiser knows how many customers will enter the subject site, estimating gross sales is simple. Numerous proprietary firms provide traffic and demographic data for locations in the United States. Traffic studies and customer capture rates can be obtained from transportation engineering firms.

Contamination Issues

Petroleum-marketing properties are apt to have contamination problems, and federal stipulations aim to ensure that contamination is contained as much as possible. The deadline for bringing all underground storage tanks (USTs) in the United States into compliance with Environmental Protection Agency standards was December 31, 1998. All older, leaking fuel storage tanks had to be replaced or decommissioned by that date. Today, all USTs are required to have monitoring equipment that alerts operators to problems.

Until the mid-1980s, most USTs consisted of bare steel, which corrodes over time and allows tank contents to leak. Congress banned the installation of unprotected steel tanks and piping in 1985. Today, all commercial retail and wholesale USTs–including all convenience store and gas station tanks–are federally regulated. Despite regulation, more than 418,000 UST releases were recorded by the

Table

3.3 Examples of Traffic Data

March 2001 Selected Transportation Trends

Hwy Num.	Mile Point	ATR Station	Location Description	Annual ADT 2000	ADT for March 2001	ADT for March 2000	Percent Change 2001/2000 March	Maximum Hour Data Day	Date	Hour	Vol.	Maximum Day Data Day	Date	Vol.
1	11.03	15-002	PACIFIC HWY., I-5, 3 mi. S of Ashland	14544	12507	13626	-8.2	SA	3	5P	1161	SA	17	14279
1	28.33	15-019	PACIFIC HWY., I-5, S of Medford Viaduct in Medford	44862	44006	42899	2.6	FR	23	4P	4088	FR	23	52874
1	42.84	15-001	PACIFIC HWY., I-5, 3 mi. W of Gold Hill	32318	31163	30753	1.3	FR	23	5P	2984	FR	23	39193
1	64.20	17-001	PACIFIC HWY., I-5, 6 mi. N of Grants Pass	20354	18869	19228	-1.9	FR	23	3P	1885	FR	23	25483
1	129.75	10-005	PACIFIC HWY., I-5, 3.40 mi. N Roseburg	29881	28361	29017	-2.3	FR	23	5P	2860	FR	23	37421

Source: Oregon Department of Transportation

United States as of September 30, 2001. Additionally, the EPA estimates that, as of March 31, 2002, there were still nearly 698,000 federally regulated USTs buried at more than 269,000 sites nationwide. Figure 3.5 shows a typical underground storage tank (UST) installation.

Contaminated UST sites vary considerably. Some are contaminated severely and have poor groundwater resources. Seriously contaminated sites require years of cleanup and remediation that can cost more than $1 million. Other sites may experience relatively minor contamination where only a small amount of the surrounding soil has been affected and no groundwater has been contaminated.

Figure

3.5 | **Underground Storage Tank Installation**

According to the Environmental Protection Agency, the average cost for site cleanup is approximately $125,000. Both UST owners and operators can be held legally responsible for cleanup and liability costs. In 1986, Congress amended Subtitle I of the Resource Conservation and Recovery Act (RCRA) to create the Leaking Underground Storage Tank (LUST) Trust Fund. The fund was established so the government could oversee site cleanup and finance the cleanup of contaminated sites where the owner or operator is unknown, unable to pay for the cleanup, or unwilling to respond.

This regulatory initiative is funded by a 0.1-cent federal tax on each gallon of motor fuel sold in the United States. The EPA has delegated most of the regulatory programs to individual states, and most states administer their UST programs through the State Department of Environmental Quality. States have the authority to implement more stringent requirements in their UST regulatory programs than federal laws require, so UST requirements vary from state to state.

A lawsuit filed by the South Tahoe Public Utility District against Shell Oil Co. and two other defendants is a prime example of how complex and costly UST contamination can be. The lawsuit focused on methyl tertiary butyl ether (MTBE) contamination of groundwater wells. The contamination was caused by USTs leaking from gas stations on the south shore of Lake Tahoe, Nev. MTBE is an additive that the oil industry introduced nationally 20 years ago. At first it was perceived by environmentalists as a valuable substance that caused gasoline to burn cleaner and produced lower atmospheric pollution levels. However, MTBE has since been found to be a major environmental hazard because it spreads rampantly when mixed with groundwater. This often happens when USTs leak gasoline containing MTBE, and the contamination problem is widespread. California has 10,000 MTBE-contaminated sites; New York has 1,500. The contamination in the South Tahoe case alone affected the drinking water of 30,000 residents. In 2002 Shell Oil Co. agreed to pay the South Tahoe Public Utility District $28 million in that lawsuit, and the total settlements awarded by the jury amounted to $69 million.

Contamination issues are complicated and costly. The typical appraiser does not have the knowledge or experience to assume liability, so environmental ratings and comments should be sought from a competent third-party expert, not the real estate appraiser. Following are suggestions on how appraisers can perform due diligence without assuming extra liability.

- The appraiser should ask owners about contamination issues, past and present, and about the presence of USTs on the property. The appraiser should be aware that this information alone is not sufficient to make any final determinations.

- The appraiser should request any environmental reports that have been prepared and read them. This is part of an appraiser's due diligence.

- The appraiser should contact the department in the subject's state that has jurisdiction over contamination issues. Usually, it is the Department of Environmental Quality. The nearest field office will have records of contamination problems for the subject site and other areas of the neighborhood.

- The appraiser should not make broad qualifying statements in the appraisal report, such as "The site appears to be environmentally clean" or "No contamination problems were found."

- Frequently, a lender or client will ask an appraiser to complete an environmental checklist or audit. These forms typically ask the appraiser for information regarding the condition of the subject site. The appraiser should only record statements of what has been observed and not offer opinions. If the appraiser cannot answer a question sufficiently, the appraiser should simply say so.

Suggested Environmental Disclosure Statement

Often, liability insurance companies and issuers of errors and omissions insurance for real estate appraisers give examples of limiting condition statements that pertain to environmental and contamination issues. Insurance companies advise appraisers to include these statements in their appraisal reports. Since convenience stores often sell petroleum products, which are a known source of environmental contamination, an appraiser should include a disclaimer in the report addressing these concerns. The disclaimer should inform the reader of the appraisal inspection's limitations regarding contamination issues. The appraiser may wish to include a statement such as the following in the appraisal report. This statement can be placed in the executive summary, assumptions and limiting conditions, or site data sections.

> The property has been used for the sale of petroleum products. The appraiser has not made a soil test or test of underground water. Identifying site and soil contaminants or environmental issues is beyond the scope of this appraisal and the appraiser's qualifications. Unless otherwise stated, this appraisal is based on the assumption that the site and property are uncontaminated and unaffected by environmentally hazardous materials or substances. No responsibility is assumed by the appraiser for contamination issues and no warranties are implied by this opinion of value. No consideration of existing or proposed regulations of the Environmental Protection Agency, nor any other government agency, has been made by the appraiser. No statement of the subject property's compliance or non-compliance with the regulations or requirements of any government agency has been made by, or implied by the appraiser. The client is advised to obtain the services of qualified environmental services contractors.

Summary

In this chapter, many convenience store criteria have been examined and examples have been given of how specific market participants rate a convenience store location. Today's convenience store business model requires that sites have excellent visibility, easy access, and sufficient land area in order to accommodate the forecourt, the building footprint, and on-site parking. Access and visibility are especially important to a convenience store's success.

The cost of convenience store sites has increased steadily over the last 20 years. As a result, rising land costs are a major concern in today's convenience store industry. Historically, fuel sales have led in-store sales in this industry, but with the entrance of mass merchandisers into the fuel sales business, that may be changing. Convenience store sales patterns may never be the same.

The next chapter examines current trends in convenience store buildings.

Chapter 4

Store Design Assessment

Petroleum-marketing properties have evolved from the small service bay gasoline stations of the 1950s and 1960s to the large convenience store markets of today. A generation ago, automotive repair services were offered where gasoline was sold. Today, car repair and maintenance services have been replaced by merchandise sales and nationally branded food service. The industry continues to change and advance. Operators are looking to the future and defining new methods for making convenience stores more appealing to customers. Chapter 4 explores those efforts.

Trends in Building Size and Development Costs

Convenience stores have grown steadily in the last 20 years. As owner-operators saw fuel profits decline, in-store sales became more important. Consequently, increasing store building size seemed logical.

As Figure 4.1 shows, the average size of an urban convenience store today is 3,620 square feet, up 40% from the average size in 1990. Convenience store buildings in rural locations historically are smaller than their urban counterparts. The average size of a rural convenience store was 3,170 square feet in 2000, a 50% increase from the average building size in 1990.

As convenience store size increased, so did building costs. Between 1990 and 2000, the average cost of building a convenience store increased by 98%, an aver-

4.1 Trends in Store Size (in Square Feet) New Urban Stores

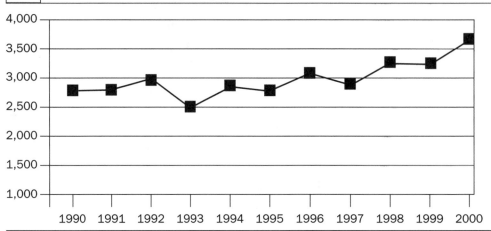

age of 9% per year. Cost increases were even more dramatic for the 20-year period from 1980 to 2000, when building costs soared 432%, or 21% annually (see Table 4.1 and Figure 4.2).

The total investment for a new urban store in 2000 was $1,860,800. That cost included the land, construction, equipment, and start-up inventory costs. The average cost breakdown for the total investment was: land, $699,800; construction, $523,200; equipment, $526,000; and start-up inventory, $111,800. On average, the cost of developing a convenience store increased 10% annually between 1990 and 2000. The most significant portion of the cost increase for new urban stores was in

Table

4.1 Cost Trends in Convenience Store Buildings

Year	Average Cost	Year	Average Cost
2000	$523,200	1999	$468,700
1998	$531,200	1997	$412,000
1996	$405,000	1995	$364,800
1994	$345,000	1993	$339,800
1992	$316,000	1991	$316,700
1990	$331,900	1989	$278,200
1987	$181,300	1986	$158,300
1985	$180,000	1984	$149,800
1983	$125,300	1982	$101,400
1981	$101,800	1980	$98,200

Source: National Association of Convenience Stores

Figure

4.2 **Cost Trends in Convenience Store Buildings**

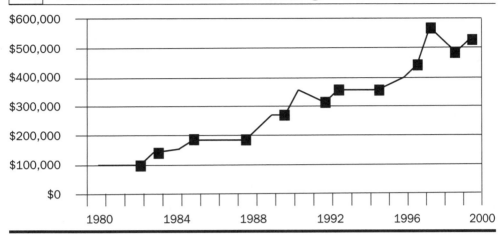

Source: National Association of Convenience Stores

land, the cost of which increased 138% over the period (see Figure 4.3). In 2000, the percentage breakdown for the various components of convenience store development was: land, 22.1%; construction, 39.9%; equipment, 32.1%; and start-up inventory, 5.9%.

Figure

4.3 **New Urban Stores: 1990-2000 Development Cost Trends**

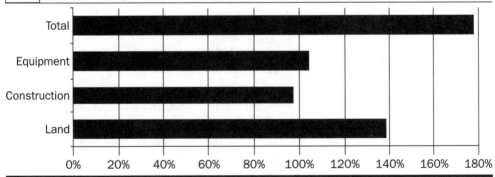

This percentage breakdown has remained fairly consistent over the last 10 years. In 2000, 3.2% of all convenience stores nationwide were remodeled at an average cost of $243,635 per store. The percentage of stores that were remodeled in 2000 had declined from the 5.0% of all stores remodeled in 1999. On average, a U.S. convenience store is remodeled every 12 years.

Basic Design Elements

With increased competitive pressure from other retail channels such as hypermarkets and drugstores, store design has become more financially important for convenience stores. Although location and cleanliness are still vital factors in attracting customers, convenience stores are moving toward broader merchandising plans to create unique identities that set them apart from other stores.

Designs must be simple enough to allow customers to access products quickly and enable owners to operate their stores efficiently. A sufficient number of checkout counters are needed to facilitate fast service, and ample parking must be provided. In newer establishments gas pumps are placed farther away from the store to promote food offerings and store products more than fuel.

If a store is to cultivate a distinct identity, signage must be consistent. Floor-to-ceiling glass windows in the front of the store are inviting and appealing to women; modern store designs allow for creativity and individuality and provide substantial curb appeal. One modern design, the "homeplate," created by the Mitchell Design Group of Irving, Texas, has become increasingly popular. Essentially, it is a triangular design in which the checkout counter is located at the rear of the store.

Technology also plays a vital role in convenience store design. According to Sun Microsystems, "The industry is heading toward convergence retailing, where the convenience center is connected to the Internet and supports services such as car washes, fast food, grocery and retail products, fuel management, kiosks, and banking."

Convenience stores generally are independently run or franchised as part of a chain. When convenience stores are affiliated with a national brand, operators must meet specific building design standards. However, new relationships between oil companies and operators are being explored that give operators more flexibility than in the past. For example, Conoco Inc. of Houston, Texas, is trying a new option—a licensed breakplace store. A *breakplace store* is one in which oil companies lend management and design assistance to store operators.

Conoco, which is striving to develop a reputation as a convenience store authority, creates an identity for a store using a few signature elements. The elements include store graphics and product "execution standards," which pertain to details such as how coffee is sold and how frequently it is brewed. Compared to a franchise, a breakplace store operates under less company control and gives operators more flexibility in local marketing.

Exterior

An appraiser will most often encounter convenience stores built with wood frame walls or concrete masonry units (CMUs). It is common to find a generic rectangular building shell with a "trade dress." A *trade dress* is something added to a building, such as a sign or logo, which indicates that a convenience store is affiliated with a well-known brand such as Shell or Exxon. Trade dress includes signage, canopy design, and a limited amount of architectural elements.

Exterior insulation finish system (EIFS), pronounced "eefs", describes an external insulation system consisting of rigid foam insulation (usually one to four inches thick) with waterproof stucco siding applied over the top. The synthetic stucco is available in 50 colors and a variety of textures. Typically, the rigid polyurethane or polystyrene insulation panels are applied over the wall studs with construction adhesive or mechanical anchors. Over the insulation, a strong fiberglass reinforcing material embedded in thick layers of base coat material is applied, strengthening the entire insulation system and providing a smooth finish. The final layer is flexible synthetic stucco, which usually is made of a tough acrylic polymer. Although it is flexible, it feels as hard as real stucco.

The EIFS colorant is mixed with the acrylic, so the coloring agent permeates the entire exterior layer of the coating. The colorant is a low-maintenance exterior finish. Surface scratches will not show and no re-painting is required. In some cases, EIFS allows the builder to reduce dimensional framing lumber from 2-in.-x-6-in. boards to 2-in.-x-4-in. boards and lower framing costs.

Aluminum composite material (ACM) panels are another common exterior material found in convenience store applications. Each panel is custom manufactured at a factory and then shipped to the site, where a contractor installs it. The industry claims that using this system, an entire building can be completed in three to five days, as opposed to the normal field fabrication time of two to three weeks. ACM panels have another benefit: they can produce rounded corners even when applied to traditional, rectangular-framed building shells (see Figure 4.4).

An oil company does not typically require specific building components in a franchise agreement. However, the company does specify the exterior colors that should be used and requires that a certain percentage of exterior wall surface be dedicated to signage.

Convenience store operators, adapting to current trends, are focusing on increasing the ornamentation on their stores' exteriors. In an effort

Figure 4.4 **ACM Panels Used in a Texaco "Star 21" Design**

to increase market share and profits, building exteriors are being designed to increase customer loyalty. The following industry news article, "Sizing Up," was published in *Convenience Store News* magazine. It describes current perceptions of convenience store design and how store owners and design consultants view their stores in relation to current industry size, layout, and design trends.

Sizing Up

With its January opening of a 7,400-square-foot convenience store, Wawa Inc. ushered in a new era of development, raising questions about the future of c-store design and merchandising, use of space and optimum store size.

The 530-unit chain has traditionally built relatively larger stores to accommodate a robust fresh-foods offering. Typical Wawa units range between 2,800 and 4,400 square feet. But the new location in Mays Landing, N.J., virtually looms over the average existing c-store, which measures 2,464 square feet, according to the 2002 CSNews Industry Report.

"The question of what size the box should be is central to the conversations I've had with several large retailers I've worked with recently," noted David Bishop, director, Willard Bishop Consulting Ltd., based in Barrington, Ill. "If you look at what some players in the industry are doing, it may indicate where some others will follow."

Customer comfort was foremost in the minds of the designers of the Mays Landing Wawa store, which, with 20 fuel positions, will serve as a template for new units in Pennsylvania and New Jersey over the next few years, noted Maureen McFadden, store design project manager for the Wawa, Pa.-based chain.

"On every level, we constantly strive to anticipate the needs of our customers and to make their lives easier," she said. "Store design is at the core of that promise."

The open floor plan offers ample customer circulation space. The unit features "sensible displays" of complementary products, with items that are often purchased together grouped throughout the store. The facility also has more storage capacity; cold beverages are housed in a 17-door cold box and fresh foods are in the center of the store.

Some see the new Wawa store as the first of many very large units to come from c-store operators. "If we look at this as a 10-year trend, we will have a lot of stores in the 7,000-, 7,500- maybe even 10,000-square-foot range," predicted Jim Mitchell of Mitchell Design Group, based in Irving, Texas. "Not all c-stores will be that way, but you will see 3,000 square feet of branded or other fresh foods added to 4,000-square-foot c-stores."

Another trend that Wawa is tapping, Mitchell said, is the re-emergence of neighborhood markets, in essence large c-stores acting as grocery stores. "The country has been aging for the last 10 years and supermarkets have been getting larger," he said. "Grandma is not going to walk through 100,000 square feet to buy the little bit of food she gets."

"At 7,400 square feet, the Wawa store may be challenging the traditional definition of convenience store," Bishop said, "but consumers will still consider the location convenient. They may be creating a separate store format that is supported in specific markets based on the demographics, geography and neighborhood, similar to Wal-Mart's Neighborhood Market strategy. They are redefining their position relative to a market, then capitalizing on a specific niche and filling it."

Over the last few years, c-store size in general has been pushed by the growing presence of gasoline, noted Coney Elliott, president of Solutions Inc., a consulting firm based in Midland, Texas. As gasoline facilities stretched from two pump positions to 10 or more, the industry's 2,400-square-foot box has been dwarfed.

"Even before the introduction of fast food inside the store," he noted, "folks were trying to make stores appear bigger to get a visual impact from the street."

More Space, Less Product

The average new c-store (less than a year old) measures 3,225 square feet, according to the 2002 CSNews Industry Report. But from a merchandising standpoint, larger stores today often have fewer products on the floor than older 2,400-square-foot stores.

"I'd say 3,000 square feet to 3,200 square feet is the minimum for new stores, with even more space added whenever additional services or product categories are added," Elliott noted. "While store size initially increased to add fast food, even retailers still offering the basic selection have increased store size to change the customer's perception.

"Some stores are designed to be more open, spacious and functional, and potentially accommodate more bulk or free-standing displays. The extra space may be used in the walk-in cooler storage, or in the fountain area, but the floor space devoted to basic products hasn't increased over the years."

Retailers are not trying to fill stores with as many products, according to Bishop, who noted that two things are evident walking into BP's newest Connect stores: There are fewer products and most are immediate consumables.

"We've seen a shift in the industry toward immediate-use products," Bishop said, "which can mean single-serve and smaller containers gaining merchandise space in some categories. For instance, 20-ounce sodas have become more visible than 12-packs of cans."

The optimal BP Connect store is 4,200 square feet, with 3,000 square feet of merchandisable area, dimensions created after considerable consumer research.

"The new stores have a wide frontage to optimize front-door parking spaces for our customers and to project street presence, showing we are in the merchandise business," said Michael O'Brien, manager of global design for London-based BP, which has U.S. offices in Chicago and New York.

"Our strategy is to provide our customers with wide aisles, lower gondolas and clear visibility to give them an easy, pleasant and efficient shopping experience."

The oil company has specific guidelines for determining the amount of space devoted to merchandising each category, to project a sense of "product authority" to customers, driving sales and margins throughout the store. An emphasis on store-operating skills ensures each unit remains uncluttered, but "it is a continual battle," he noted.

Smaller stores of 2,400 square feet and less cannot provide the same shopping experience, O'Brien commented, "but we are doing our best to upgrade the retail skills, capabilities and product offerings to give the best shopping experience within our smaller stores."

In some units this could mean eliminating subcategories to give the customer a clear, uncluttered choice within core categories. "The number of product SKUs is tightly managed within each store size by planograms," explained Richard Griffin, BP's vice president of marketing, central business unit. "We pay a lot of attention to SKU count discipline."

Returns on site and store investment are carefully managed by BP, he added. "We have a rigorous process and high return expectations. We are continually working at building more efficiently to drive down unnecessary costs and look for new ways of presenting our customers with the same standards. We also are continually looking at ways to drive our merchandise intensity within the store to drive sales and margin efficiencies."

Bigger Not Always Better

While operators like Wawa have an established, destination food service business or other retail driver, larger formats aren't a guarantee of larger sales or profits, industry players caution. "Some retailers built a few [newly designed, larger] stores and spent $300 per square foot—they were never going to make money off those darn things," said Ian Rattray, vice president, senior project director, for Miller Zell, the Atlanta-based design consulting firm that created Sunoco Inc.'s new, award-winning A-Plus design. "Good design really makes money. It's got to bring a return on investment."

Redesigns can look better and be more efficient, while costing less than a retailer's current new builds, he noted. "Image does not necessarily mean more money," Rattray said, noting retailers who have larger stores in mind should analyze the costs associated with traditional brick-and-mortar construction; pre-manufactured, modular buildings; and pre-engineered buildings that are put together like giant Erector sets, which may be less costly, especially in union areas.

"You need to look at the store in totality, making what the customer feels and sees better, at less cost," he said.

In some instances, c-store operators have tried to compete through their facility, rather than execution, Elliott added. "You can't sell the look of the store. The facility will attract, but not hold the customer. You've got to have the right location, product offering, price and personality to be successful. Some people have invested excessive dollars into building monuments to themselves or the community or for whatever reason. In many cases, those have not succeeded because they were not functional or didn't have the right product offering."

A number of successful c-store operators, such as QuikTrip Inc. and Love's Country Stores, have not substantially increased the size of their stores, but have continued to modify the basic rectangle, upgrade merchandising and expand their primary offering, such as fountain drinks and coffee, Elliott noted. "They build nice, modern facilities that are appealing, but are not monuments," he said. "They have stayed traditional when it comes to store design, but have enhanced location, overall presentation and product. Some folks are putting dollars in people and location, as well as facility. Others tend to put it only in facility."

At Oak Brook, Ill.-based Clark Retail Enterprises Inc., which operates units from 300 to more than 3,000 square feet, as well as a 7,500-square-foot truckstop, facility size is tied to the store brand, the nature of that brand's offerings and the space required to merchandise each item. Clark's Oh Zone! stores are more than 2,800 square feet in size; White Hen stores are 2,000 to 2,400 square feet or greater; On the Go units range from 300 to 3,000 square feet.

"Location dictates the offering," said John Matthews, vice president of marketing and facilities. "Where we have the opportunity to control size, we attempt to do so. We have target spacing for each of the brands, but store size is generally dictated to us, unless we are doing a ground-up.

"C-stores generally don't offer the luxury of creating vast allotments of space. We find if you design a merchandising set for the smallest stores, you can enlarge the set or add incremental sets to your large stores in a modular fashion. There is a tendency to squeeze as much in as possible, while allowing for all the necessary ADA [Americans with Disabilities Act] requirements. If space were not as much of a constraint, we would instill customer queuing and resting areas in the store to enhance the overall experience."

While others are sizing up, one of Clark's newest store concepts—for office buildings—requires only 2,000 square feet. "We would like to have more, but where we put this concept—generally high-rise buildings—it becomes cost-prohibitive to go much larger due to rents. Therefore, we make 2,000 work."

Making Over the Small Box

Regardless of how many retailers start building 3,500- or 4,500- or even 10,000-square-foot stores, the majority of c-store locations are still in the area of 2,400 square feet. While few retailers do wholesale retrofits, many are making changes to present a more spacious feeling, including reducing SKUs and reconfiguring gondola runs.

"The industry average is 3,200 SKUs [per store]," Bishop said. "But you will see stores today going below 2,000 SKUs and in some cases 1,500. That opens space in smaller stores and begs the question, what do we do with all this free space? It gets to reinventing the store and how some retailers are defining their markets more narrowly."

Mitchell is involved in a number of remerchandising efforts with retailers looking for ways to open up the traditional c-store. "We reduce shelving, but not product offering," he said. "Many retailers are not paying attention to what is on the shelf. They may have two or three sizes of bleach, two brands of dishwashing fluid, maybe in different sizes. If we reduced some of these to one SKU in a medium size, we won't lose sales, but can reduce the amount of shelving."

What's more, most retailers usually buy shelving that is too deep and don't use vertical space efficiently, said Mitchell, who recommends a flexible system of wire shelving and slat board, where shelving can be adjusted horizontally and vertically. "Go over to the shelf that holds groceries or paper products, squat down and look at it straight on from the end. You will see about 20 percent of the space is not used, especially height-wise and depth-wise. Retailers are spending money on shelving they don't need. I can go into almost any store in the country and take out 8 feet of shelving, but put 10 percent more product in it."

A-Plus for Design

Sunoco's A-Plus design for its new 4,200-square-foot stores was used to retrofit more than 400 smaller existing locations before the first new build broke ground; it has now been used to retrofit more than 500 stores. "You are trying to get an impact in the marketplace with any new brand development," said Miller Zell's Rattray. "To do a new build and expect that to carry the day, just won't happen. The new design acts as a catalyst for the right thing to happen at the 500, 3,000 or 10,000 locations already there. That's when you get the brand into the marketplace and have an impact on sales, margins and profits."

With the new A-Plus, the designer wasn't looking only to increase the footprint. The total volume of the store—the sense of space, increased height, etc.—was important.

"Based on our consumer research, we wanted to give the store the feel of a marketplace," Rattray said. "In many ways, people have a negative impression of c-stores. Having the sense of openness and security helps draw people in from the forecourt into the backcourt."

Added David Kotke, vice president of marketing for Miller Zell: "There are specific avenues of retailing we think have trailed all of the trends—and any woman would know that. The oil industry is one of those. The majority of stores are cold and industrial looking with a sheet of bulletproof glass. We have to bust a paradigm, and that need to bust out is driving the height and sense of volume in the store."

Clean and Simple

The visual clutter in the typical c-store can be broken in a larger store, helping customers focus on a specific product segment. "One way to do that is to give a larger volume and to simplify communication in the store. It makes the space feel less cramped and easier to shop," said Rattray

In the new A-Plus design, each primary product category—cold beverages, fountain, tobacco, food service—has its own "storefront" with a distinct, but complementary feel. The cooler area, for instance, has a lower ceiling and change of color of the tile. "We wanted that area of the store to feel like a traditional c-store," he said. "It makes the food service side of the store more unusual and reinforces it."

Merchandise is raised up off the floor in many cases, thereby cross-merchandised at eye-level. "While getting coffee, a customer will see a Twinkie at eye level," Rattray noted.

To retrofit this spacious image and "company brand," Sunoco took key parts, refined them and put them in the existing store base. In the tobacco category, for instance, the department is branded and given a defined planogram, making its presence substantial. Then, depending on the size of the store, the department fluctuates from 6 feet to 16 feet. "But the brand image is maintained," he said, adding that "the skillful paring down of SKUs to get to the right level of offering is definitely the trend and will open the store up."

Cosmetically, simple things can be done to retrofit older stores to make them feel bigger and bring a sense of consistency to newer, larger stores in a chain. "A lot of it has to do with cleaning up the location and doing things as simple as putting in new floor tile," Rattray said. "While the designs are not exactly the same, the general feel is the same."

Summed up Kotke: "Being able to maintain store imagery is critical. This industry has struggled with that."

Interior

A convenience store's interior floor area is usually classified in two ways: as sales area—the area of the store where products are sold—and non-sales area—the area of the store that is occupied by equipment, storage, etc. Today, sales areas occupy approximately 70% of a store's total floor area.

Many nationally branded oil companies and fast food chains have off-the-shelf floor plans available to assist prospective convenience store developers in planning their projects. Below is an example of an off-the-shelf design for a convenience store with a full-sized McDonald's restaurant. This concept is called a "2-in-1."

Figure 4.6 shows a diagram of a McDonald's USA rural concept convenience store. A generic floor plan such as this allows appraisers to observe several common modern convenience store design features. Each area in the diagram is described below.

Figure 4.6 Generic Convenience Store Floor Plan—McDonald's USA Rural Concept

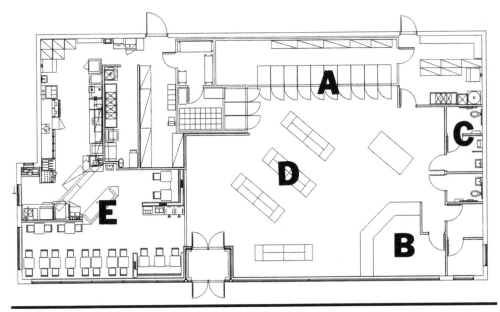

Source: McDonald's USA Web site

Area A. The beverage coolers and high-demand items such as beer, milk, and bread are usually placed at the back of the store to encourage customers to pass by other merchandise and make "impulse buys," which can account for 70% of store sales. The average new convenience store today has 37 linear feet of walk-in cooler space. Experienced operators say that a 10-foot-wide cooler is much more efficient for stocking than the standard 8-foot-wide design. If a new owner-operator's plans for a new store call for an 8-foot-wide cooler, the appraiser should inform the owner of this potential design problem.

Area B. The checkout area is located where the clerk can see all parts of the store interior and the fueling area; theft is a major concern in this industry.

Area C. Eighty-five percent of new stores have ADA-compliant restrooms. Noncompliant public restrooms not only are a form of functional obsolescence, they are also illegal. It is important for convenience store operators to keep their stores' restrooms clean. Customers rank clean restrooms as the fourth most important store characteristic on surveys of why they shop at convenience stores.

Area D. Gondolas are free-standing shelves for merchandise display. The highest margin items are usually placed at eye level. The endcaps are considered high-visibility locations. Gondolas are equipment and not part of the real estate.

Area E. One of the latest convenience store trends is full-size, branded fast-food restaurants, which replace the smaller, express units that were tried a few years ago. Indoor seating and separate entrances are now required by many fast-food chains.

Adequate security continues to be a priority for convenience store owners and operators; good security not only protects employees and customers, but also limits employer liability and prevents company loss. The National Association of Convenience Stores (NACS) urges convenience store operators to use three basic strategies to curb crime:

1. Train employees to prevent crime.
2. Establish systems to control cash.
3. Ensure that stores are visible and well lighted.

Advanced technology contributes to the effectiveness of these strategies. Technological security methods include closed-circuit television systems, 24-hour video recorders, and silent alarm systems (including a remote alarm that employees can carry on their necks, on belts, or in pockets). An interactive security system enables owners to monitor up to four stores remotely at one time. An interactive security system may use monitors, cameras, microphones, and video software. Two-way video systems can monitor third-shift workers remotely and ensure that there is no trouble during off hours. Sophisticated safes have features that require the person who keys in the combination to wait 10 minutes before opening the safe. Bullet-resistant glass windows and check-out enclosures provide another level of security, although bullet-resistant does not mean bulletproof.

Employee theft can be tracked using technology as well. Pinhole cameras can monitor employee activities, and some "smart safes" actually count the money, which not only deters employee theft but also reduces bank charges.

Some establishments have attracted law enforcement officials to their stores by providing free coffee or a place to do paperwork. Thirty-one Circle K stores have gone a step further by placing telephones, fax machines, and work stations in their stores for police officers to use.

Food Service Operations

The earliest branded quick-serve restaurants (QSRs) were smaller "express" units within convenience stores that often had limited menus. Many of them failed to meet industry expectations, however. Today, most national chains prefer to attach a full restaurant to a convenience store, with full trade dress and exterior signage. These facilities often are developed jointly by the convenience store operator and the QSR. A QSR's ownership structure varies. Sometimes the QSR owns and operates the restaurant and common area expenses are shared; in other cases, the QSR leases shell space from the convenience store operator. Some chains refuse to franchise with convenience stores, preferring to operate the units independently.

Co-Branding Allows Sharing of Development Costs and Operating Expenses

When a restaurant and convenience store locate on the same parcel, this co-branding reduces land costs significantly and may reduce a building's development costs as well. Co-branding may allow a convenience store to locate at a site that otherwise would be too costly. Square footage requirements for branded food service vary, from 1,000 square feet to 2,500 square feet for full restaurants to minimal dedicated counter space for pizza and snack operations. Half of the major hamburger chains require full-size restaurants. Notably, burger chains need 1,700 square feet of space, the highest average space requirements of all fast-food restaurants. Sandwich concept stores are typically 1,025 square feet in size, while *convenience store specialists*, food service programs designed specifically for convenience stores, require the smallest amount of space, averaging only 200 square feet.

Appraisers are responsible for knowing a co-branded restaurant's hours of operation and if breakfast, lunch, and dinner are all served. Drive-thru lanes should be positioned on the side of the store most visible to potential customers; they should never be located at the back of the store.

Additional Profit Centers

With intense competition from hypermarkets and drugstores, new business concepts are being explored that someday could change the design of convenience stores entirely. As never before, operators are searching for ways to motivate customers to spend more, and they are using *additional profit centers (APCs)* to do so. APCs are new concepts that are incorporated into a store's design in addition to fuel and merchandise. As the industry changes, APCs may be redefined by excluding poorly performing concepts and adding new ideas that are not evident today. The most common APCs being discussed in the industry are listed below. APCs have not yet proven to be economically viable, however.

Products	Services
Fresh deli/brand fast food	Pharmacy/drugs
Nutritional snack/energy bars	Carwash
Enhanced beverage selection	Car care center
Enhanced snack selection	Vacuum/air
Video rental	Attendant
	Copy/fax services
	Stamps/mail center
	Dry cleaning pick-up/drop off
	Post office/mailing centers
	Photo processing
	Insert banks/drive-thru banks
	Travel agencies/ticket sales

Appraisers also should be aware of industry marketing trends at this crucial time in the convenience store industry. Convenience store designs could change radically in a few years, depending on which APCs thrive. The convenience store industry recognizes that fundamental changes in retailing are on the horizon, so planning for new design concepts is underway.

Sources of Data

Local architects specializing in convenience stores

McDonald's USA Web site
Contains specific site criteria for small towns and urban locations
www.mcdonalds.com/countries/usa/corporate/index.html

Classic Industries
Manufactures aluminum composite panels for convenience store applications.
http://www.classicusa.com

Chapter 5

Fuel Service and Canopy Assessment

In many respects, convenience stores have characteristics similar to quick-service restaurants and drugstores. However, unlike quick-service restaurants and drugstores, convenience stores have fuel service. The term *fuel service* refers to the improvements used in the dispensing and sale of retail motor fuel. Fuel service includes the underground storage tanks (USTs), dispensers, canopies, electronics, and piping. Although it was not the case in the past, today the industry considers these improvements to be part of the real estate. Fuel service is considered to be a separate category of improvements from the convenience store building, carwash, or other improvements. Typically, the appraiser includes all these items in the appraisal of the convenience store's real estate.

Convenience store appraisers must be able to describe and analyze fuel service components. Much of the information in Chapter 5 is provided by the National Institute of Standards and Technology. The chapter explains how the fuel service operates and describes the latest technological innovations found in new convenience stores. It begins by exploring the terminology used in today's convenience store industry. Convenience store appraisers must understand the terms *retail motor fuel* and *fuel dispenser* and use them correctly to maintain their credibility.

Retail motor fuel describes the products convenience stores typically sell. Gasoline is a specific type of fuel and should not be confused with diesel fuel, which is an entirely different product. Gasoline and diesel fuel are never mixed and separate dispensing devices are used for each. The term *motor fuel* can also include gasohol, kerosene, and blended fuels, which are becoming more common.

The term *fuel dispenser* describes the device that dispenses fuel into a vehicle. The device is no longer called a gas pump and, as this chapter explains, some dispensers do not even have an internal pump. A convenience store appraiser should never refer to a diesel dispenser as a *diesel gas pump*. Gas and diesel are not the same thing, and the device may not be a pump at all. The appraiser is expected to know such differences.

A motor fuel dispenser, also called a *motor fuel device*, is designed to measure and deliver liquids used as fuel for internal-combustion engines. The term *retail motor fuel device* is a specific category of dispenser, and the difference between a retail dispenser and a wholesale dispenser is significant. A retail dispenser is used for single fuel deliveries of less than 100 gallons, retail fuel deliveries to individual highway vehicles, and single deliveries of liquefied petroleum gas for domestic use and liquefied petroleum gas or liquid anhydrous ammonia for non-resale use. Wholesale devices, on the other hand, deliver large quantities of fuel that will be resold. A fuel device used to measure gasoline before it is delivered to a convenience store is considered a wholesale device because the gasoline will be sold again.

Fuel Dispensing System

A fuel dispensing system's design depends on numerous factors, including a facility's size and volume of business; the number of different grades, blends, or separate fuel products it sells; and the desirability of features such as self service, remote cashiers, prepayment, and multi-tier pricing. *Multi-tier pricing* means that one type of fuel is sold at more than one price per gallon, depending on the delivery or payment method. Whether complex or simple, retail fuel dispensing systems have three basic components: storage tanks, pipelines, and dispensers. These components are shown in Figure 5.1.

Storage Tanks

Most storage tanks at retail fuel facilities are installed under ground so they will be shielded from extreme temperature variations, fire, and vehicles moving through the gas station (see Figure 5.2). Underground storage tanks also allow aboveground space to be used efficiently, and land can be especially valuable in urban areas. However, maintenance, leak detection, containment, and cleanup are much easier when tanks are aboveground. Consequently, changes in federal environmental protection regulations may encourage convenience stores to install aboveground storage tanks in the future.

Whether aboveground or belowground tanks are used, each type of fuel a convenience store sells is stored in a separate tank, except at stations that use special

Figure

5.1 | **Basic Components of a Fuel Dispensing System**

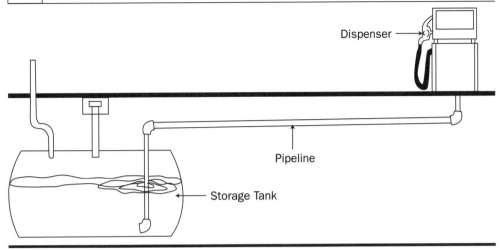

Source: National Institute of Standards and Technology, Gaithersburg, Md. 20899.

equipment to produce blended fuel. A storage tank's size depends on the amount of available space and the retailer's needs. Large storage tanks hold as much as 12,000 gallons of fuel–slightly more than 1,600 cubic feet.

When a storage tank is filled, the rising liquid level pressurizes air and vapor in the upper portion of the tank. Excessive pressure can strain the tank and cause it to leak. A pressure deficiency also can strain the pumping mechanism, make delivery through the system impossible, or cause vaporization in delivery lines. To prevent these problems, storage tanks have vent pipes that allow pressure in the tank to be maintained at a desirable level–usually slightly above atmospheric pressure. Keeping the air pressure in the UST at a slightly higher level than the surrounding atmospheric pressure prevents contaminants from entering the fuel delivery system. The vent line generally is equipped with a relief valve, which opens at the preset

Figure 5.2 | **Diagram of an Underground Storage Tank**

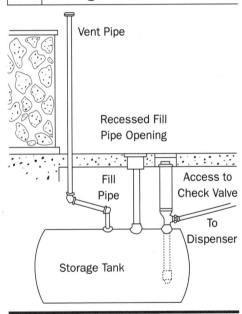

Source: National Institute of Standards and Technology.

pressure to allow air and vapor to be released from the tank into the atmosphere. The relief valve also allows air to be drawn into the tank from the atmosphere.

Environmental protection laws in many states mandate that fuel-dispensing equipment have vapor recovery systems. *Vapor recovery systems* balance pressure between discharging tanks and receiving tanks, thus preventing vapor from escaping into the atmosphere.

Storage tanks are filled periodically by tanker trucks. A fill pipe (see Figure 5.3) extends from the underground tank to a level just below the pavement's surface, where the pipe is accessible but protected from vehicles moving through the station. To ensure that the proper fuel type is delivered to the convenience store, fill pipes must be clearly labeled or color-coded. They also must be capped securely to avoid contamination from dirt and moisture. In many states, overfill containment is required for fill pipes underground. A box surrounding the pipe captures gasoline that overflows when a delivery truck pours too much gasoline into the underground storage tank.

Figure

5.3   **Diagram of a Self-Contained Pump System**

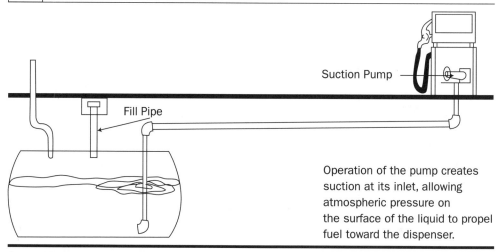

Suction Pump

Fill Pipe

Operation of the pump creates suction at its inlet, allowing atmospheric pressure on the surface of the liquid to propel fuel toward the dispenser.

Source: National Institute of Standards and Technology.

Pipelines

Fuel travels from a storage tank to a dispenser through underground pipelines. To avoid contacting vehicles near the service island, pipelines rise to the surface of the land directly below dispensers. They must be carefully designed and installed to minimize fuel leakage. A single storage tank can serve several dispensers, so pipelines may be extensive. The temperature of the soil near the surface is similar to the temperature of the surrounding air, but the underground temperature will be different. Pipelines extending from the underground storage tanks to the dispensers must be positioned in a way that minimizes any temperature difference. Fuel traveling from a cold storage tank through warmer pipelines can vaporize, resulting in *vapor lock*, which prevents fuel from reaching its destination. Vapor lock often occurs in improperly installed fuel dispensing systems. Fuel is especially apt to vaporize in self-contained dispensers, which are described below.

Dispensers

The dispenser is the heart of the fuel delivery system and the component an appraiser should be most concerned with when conducting field inspections. There are different types of dispensers, and appraisers should accurately describe the dispensers found at the subject property and comparable properties in their reports. Dispensers have a variety of control mechanisms that regulate the fuel delivery rate, prevent overfill and siphoning, and ensure that the components that register volume and price are reset to zero at the beginning of each delivery. As the device dispenses fuel, it measures the fuel volume and calculates its price. The most common types of dispensers are self-contained pumps and remote pumps, dual-product dispensers, and multi-product dispensers. Descriptions of each follow.

Self-Contained and Remote Pumps. When fuel is stored in tanks below fuel dispensers, it must be brought to the surface against the force of gravity. This is accomplished in one of two ways. The fuel can be pulled toward the dispenser by a *self-contained pump* (also called a *suction pump*) located in the dispenser unit, as shown in Figure 5.3, or the fuel can be pushed toward the dispenser by a *remote pump* located in the storage tank, as shown in Figure 5.4. A self-contained pump draws fuel from the storage tank; a remote pump pushes fuel out of the storage tank. Remote pumps are often called *remote dispensers*. While retailers use both types of dispensing systems, most new installations are equipped with remote dispensers.

Both self-contained pump and remote pump systems have advantages and disadvantages. When one storage tank serves several single-product dispensers, a remote pump system is useful because a single pump supplies fuel to the entire system. Throughout the system's life, a single pump will require less maintenance than several separate pumps will. In a multi-dispenser system like the one shown in Figure 5.5, the remote pump seems to have a clear advantage. However, if the pump breaks, the entire system will have to be taken out of service while repairs are made.

In a self-contained pump system, on the other hand, each dispenser has its own pump and operates independently. If one dispenser malfunctions, the other dispensers continue to operate.

Figure

| 5.4 | **A Remote Dispenser System**

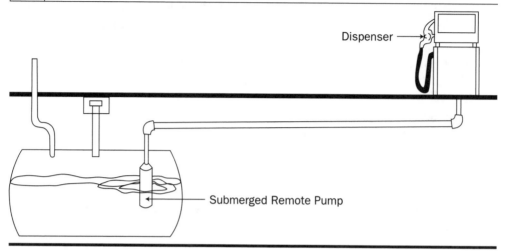

Source: National Institute of Standards and Technology.

Figure

| 5.5 | **Comparison of a Remote Dispenser (left) and a Self-Contained Pump System (right)**

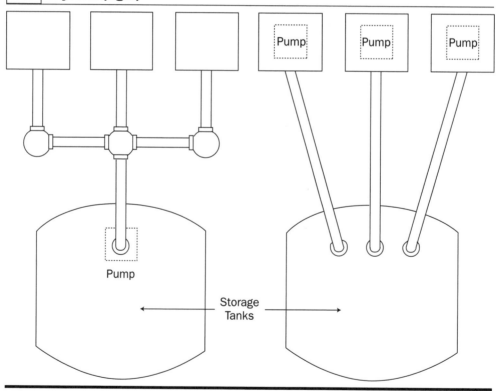

Source: National Institute of Standards and Technology.

Dual-Product Dispensers. Most convenience stores sell several types of fuel, including unleaded gasoline, diesel fuel, gasohol, and kerosene. Gasoline is available in various grades, including regular, premium, and blended varieties. Each fuel type can be stored in a separate tank and transported to dispensers through separate pipelines.

The dual-product dispensers shown in Figure 5.6 have two separate mechanical structures located within one shell. If each dispenser delivers the same fuel type, the unit is called a *single-product dispenser*, or a *one-dual*. If a dispenser delivers different fuel types, it may be called a *two-product dual dispenser*, or *two-dual*, *twin*, or *duo*.

Figure

| 5.6 | **One-Product and Two-Product Dual Dispensers** |

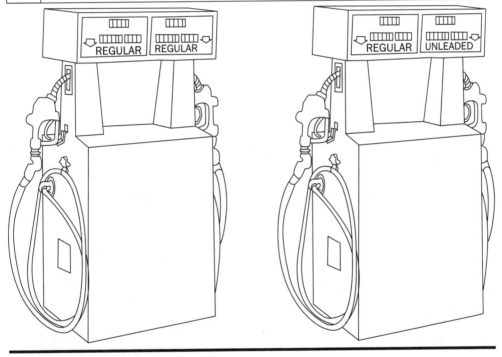

Source: National Institute of Standards and Technology.

Single-product dual dispensers may share a single pump and, thus, a single pipeline connection, as shown in Figure 5.7. This reduces the number of suction pumps needed, but each dispenser must be equipped with its own control valve so that it can operate independently. In two-product dual dispensers, each dispenser is independent and has its own components and pipeline connection. Figure 5.8 shows two types of dual dispensers that appraisers typically encounter.

Figure

5.7

A Single-Product Dual Dispenser

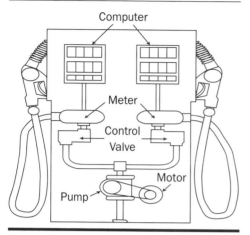

Source: National Institute of Standards and Technology.

Multiple-Product Dispensers (MPDs). The multiple-product dispenser (MPD) is the most popular type of dispenser among retailers. It has been popular for several years, especially in large fueling outlets. Retailers favor MPDs because several fuel grades can be selected from the two, three, or four hoses on one dispenser. A set of electronics and a computer control all of the hoses on one side of the fuel dispenser. A recent variation on the multiple-product dispenser is the "single-hose" version, through which all fuel grades merge into a *manifold,* a mechanical device that allows several pipes to join into one and supply a single hose.

Figure

5.8 **Two Typical Dual-Product Dispensers**

Multiple-product dispensers may be designed in either self-contained or remote pump versions, and each fuel grade has its own hydraulic system. Figure 5.9 shows the exterior of several multiple-product dispensers from different manufacturers. The interior configurations of the piping systems are shown in Figure 5.10. Although Figure 5.10 is useful for understanding fuel dispensers' complex inner workings, appraisers do not typically remove the covering to inspect a fuel dispenser's interior.

While dispensers have different physical characteristics, their basic operations are similar. Federal safety regulations require that people using any type of dispenser take the extra step of pushing a button, rotating a lever, or lifting a handle.

Blended Fuel Dispensers. Blended fuels are created by blending different grades of fuel at the pump. A high-octane grade of fuel and a low-octane grade of fuel can be mixed to produce a blended grade of fuel. Modern blended fuel dispensers can produce as many as five grades of gasoline. However, leaded and unleaded gasoline cannot be mixed.

Fuel retailers have offered blended fuels for many years at both single- and multiple-product dispensers. Retailers prefer blended fuel dispensers to single-product

Figure

5.9 | Exterior of Multiple-Product Dispensers from Different Manufacturers

Figure

5.10 | Internal View of a Multiple-Product Dispenser

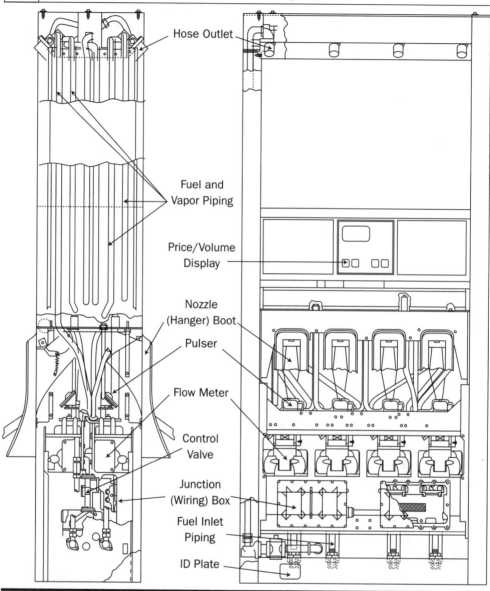

Hose Outlet

Fuel and
Vapor Piping

Price/Volume
Display

Nozzle
(Hanger) Boot

Pulser

Flow Meter

Control
Valve

Junction
(Wiring) Box

Fuel Inlet
Piping

ID Plate

dispensers because they require fewer separate underground storage tanks. A *multi-hose* dispenser has one hose for each fuel type. Figures 5.11 through 5.14 illustrate various types of blended fuel dispensers. Figure 5.11 depicts a three-hose blended fuel dispenser. Figure 5.12 shows a system that has a single hose for all three products. This type of dispenser has a fixed-ratio blender configuration, which dispenses blended fuel at only one setting for octane content. Figure 5.13 represents single- and multi-hose arrangements for several blended fuel types. Figure 5.14 shows a system with one hose for blended fuel and another hose for diesel.

Mechanical and Electronic Fuel Dispensers

Retail fuel dispensers are classified as either mechanical or electronic. A fuel dispenser's classification is determined by the mechanism that registers the sale price and number of gallons of fuel dispensed. All mechanisms are either analog or digital. Analog mechanisms are used in old, mechanical dispensers, while digital mechanisms are used in modern, electronic dispensers.

Mechanical Dispensers. Mechanical systems typically are used in small or old retail outlets and have analog indicators. Their volume and price indicators are usually revolving wheels–one for each digit–as shown in Figure 5.15. While fuel is being delivered, the wheels for the smallest amounts (usually cents for price and tenths of a gallon for volume) move continuously. The fuel delivered is being measured and its price computed continuously, even though the amounts are not precise in the spaces between whole numbers. For example, the purchase price indicated in Figure 5.15 is between $14.06 and $14.07.

The precision with which a mechanical dispenser calculates the customer's purchase price is limited by the size and markings on the wheel. Typically, the smallest fraction is one cent, so mechanical dispensers cannot register a total price that includes fractional amounts, such as tenths of a cent.

Figure 5.11 **Three-Hose Blended Fuel Dispenser**

Figure 5.12 **System with Single Hose for Three Products**

Figure 5.13 Single- and Multi-Hose Arrangements for Several Blended Fuel Types

Figure 5.14 System with Hoses for High-Octane Fuel and Blended Fuel

Electronic Dispensers. Most new fuel dispensing systems are electronic. Unlike mechanical dispensers, electronic dispensers have digital indicators, as shown in Figure 5.16. Digital indicators (usually liquid crystal or LED displays) quickly "jump" from one price to the next. Measurements are precise and are always shown in whole numbers.

Electronic systems are more efficient than mechanical dispensers. They have fewer internal moving parts, require less maintenance, and can accurately register fuel deliveries in amounts as small as thousandths of a gallon or tenths of one cent. They can also be adapted to record metric measurement and a sale price in foreign currency.

Electronic systems allow for multi-tier pricing and can be connected to electronic input and output devices such as remote readouts and data storage, management, and communication systems. Using such devices, an attendant can control numerous dispensers simultaneously from a remote location such as an enclosed cashier's station. Readouts show each dispenser's operating status, the amount of fuel delivered, the price per gallon, and the total price.

In some electronic systems, the operator can set self-service pumps to deliver a specific amount of fuel, determined either by total price or volume, so that customers can pay before filling the tank. Many electronic systems can record store sales data by product and sale type (cash/credit card). The data can then be stored electronically at the convenience store or transmitted directly to a central data storage facility located across town or in another city. Thus, the system becomes a valuable business management tool.

With their modern features, electronic fuel dispensing systems can substantially reduce labor costs, especially at large facilities. Because most electronic systems have modular designs, features can be added without replacing existing equipment.

Advances in Technology

Recent technological improvements in dispensers allow customers to pay for fuel quickly and easily. The most common customer payment method today is "pay-at-the-pump," or point-of-sale (POS) payment. Surveys show that 65% of stores now have pay-at-the-pump technology. With this type of payment system, credit or debit card readers are installed at the dispenser. The customer can complete the purchase by swiping the credit or debit card through the card reader. The payment is received and a receipt is printed at the dispenser, so customers do not even have to enter the store. Some industry reports show that fuel sales increase 30% with POS credit card readers. Pay-at-the-pump technology is convenient for customers and makes employees' jobs easier. POS credit card readers are also appealing to convenience store operators because they can hire fewer employees.

Figure 5.15 **Analog Indicator**

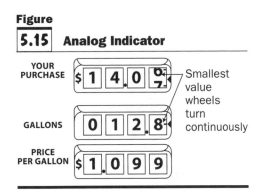

YOUR PURCHASE $1 4 0 0 7 — Smallest value wheels turn continuously

GALLONS 0 1 2 8

PRICE PER GALLON $1 0 9 9

Figure 5.16 **Digital Indicator on Electronic Dispenser**

When a convenience store operator markets fuel at a low price, fuel sales can increase. However, pay-at-the-pump technology discourages customers from buying in-store items. As a result, pay-at-the-pump sales have increased in recent years while beverage and other store sales have plummeted.

To compensate for reduced merchandise sales, new dispensers are being designed to draw customers into the store, where high-margin sales occur. In 1999–2000, Gilbarco, a fuel dispenser manufacturer based in Greensboro, N.C., introduced a dispenser that has a video display and slim design (see Figure 5.17). The

Figure 5.17 Fuel Dispenser with Video Display and Slim Design

video display allows for POS advertising and cross-merchandising, and the narrow design improves visibility.

Alternative noncash payment methods also are being introduced into the convenience store market. Prepaid cards, automobile decals, and key chains with computer chips that act as encoded electronic billing devices are being tested in markets nationwide. In Shell USA's test market program, the customer does not have to leave the car to pay for gasoline; the fueling is completely automated. A robotic arm moves the fuel hose to a gas cap on the customer's car and an electronic reader recognizes the payment from a computer chip decal on the windshield. Technology that allows customers to pay by using a finger scan that reads the customer's fingerprint also is being tested. Customers whose payment is tied to a debit card or checking account, however, must sign a receipt.

As new technology is introduced, old dispensers are becoming obsolete and decreasing in value. An old component may be functionally obsolete even though it still works. For example, it is impossible to convert a mechanical dispenser to current pay-at-the-pump technology. The convenience store operator will have to replace the mechanical dispenser entirely even though it is doing what it was designed to do.

Canopies

Canopies are considered part of the fuel service and, therefore, part of the real estate. They have four basic components: the frame, which is typically steel; the skin, which is usually enamel-coated steel or aluminum composite material (ACM);

the lighting; and the signage. Between 1990 and 2000, the average cost of the fuel service and canopy increased by 90%, an average of 8% per year. From 1980 to 2000, the cost increased by 697%, an average annual increase of 33% per year. See Table 5.1 and Figure 5.18.

Table

5.1	Cost Trends in Fuel Service and Canopies		
Year	**Average Cost**	**Year**	**Average Cost**
2000	$292,600	1989	$118,300
1999	$232,300	1988	$84,500
1998	$331,100	1987	$84,900
1997	$206,300	1986	$88,000
1996	$238,700	1985	$65,700
1995	$211,100	1984	$55,100
1994	$228,100	1983	$59,900
1993	$219,200	1982	$46,300
1992	$200,500	1981	$48,800
1991	$173,100	1980	$36,700
1990	$153,900		

Figure

| 5.18 | Cost Trends in Fuel Service and Canopies |

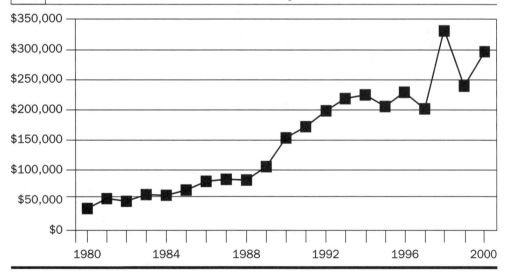

Source: National Association of Convenience Stores.

Canopy Design

A canopy gives a convenience store an identity and can be a petroleum marketer's signature element. Canopies come in many shapes and sizes and can be pre-engineered or custom built for a specific site. They are an asset to convenience stores because they provide shelter and can effectively advertise a brand through their color and design. A convenience store that does not have a canopy today is considered functionally obsolete. When valuing a convenience store, the appraiser should note the convenience store's structural design and fueling capacity and indicate whether the canopy adequately accommodates the site's fueling design.

Good fueling positions that allow vehicles to be fueled simultaneously are critical to a convenience store's success. Generally, each dispenser has one fueling position on each side. A convenience store should have enough fueling positions to accommodate peak traffic volume. Two of the most common fueling designs are shown in Figures 5.19 and 5.20.

A canopy's design and shape should be appropriate for the fueling configuration. The configuration can be either a "starting gate" design or a "four-square" design. Figure 5.19 shows a four-square design, although it is not square and has more than four dispensers. In this configuration, it may be difficult for some customers to access the dispensers if the dispensers in the drive path are being used. Figure 5.20 shows a starting gate design, which is the most popular canopy configuration in the industry. Unlike the four-square design, customers can access each dispenser without being blocked by other customers. Consequently, starting gate designs are effectively able to accommodate peak volume.

Note that Figure 5.20 shows six fueling positions. In 2000 convenience stores had an average of 8.6 fueling positions, but that figure is declining as convenience store operators focus on high-margin in-store sales.

A gable design has a two-sided, sloping pitched roof similar to the roof on a house. Although the design is practical,

Figure

5.19 **Four-Square Design**

Figure

5.20 **Starting Gate Design**

gable canopies are expensive to build and are used mostly on convenience stores in areas that receive heavy snowfall.

Some fuel retailers have tried to increase their brand recognition by using atypical canopy designs such as the one shown in Figure 5.21. However, unusual canopy designs often are more expensive to install than typical canopy designs and in a competitive market the investment may not increase sales and profits.

According to Sharpline Converting, a canopy design firm, local signage ordinances put restrictions on canopy designs. To reduce glare in residential areas, some local signage ordinances forbid stores from having backlighting. In residential areas, lighting at nearby businesses can affect the design of a convenience store's exterior signs and lights. "Light contamination" is a growing concern among many local government planning and zoning boards. Nearly every jurisdiction today has some type of restriction and the appraiser should know how canopy restrictions affect a convenience store's ability to advertise in a certain location.

Canopy Structure

Appraisers should note exposed steel and a canopy's poor drainage in their valuations. Exposed steel is an ongoing maintenance problem because it rusts and can shorten a canopy's life. Because canopies have large surface areas, adequate drainage is crucial. In addition, a canopy's structural steel can last indefinitely. The "skin" or surfaces such as the parapets (a canopy's vertical surfaces) might need to be replaced several times over the canopy's life. "Re-skinning" is usually required with a brand change. Canopies do not have much salvage value and when structural steel is welded onsite it becomes difficult to dismantle and move to another location.

Figure

5.21 **Unusual Canopy Design**

Summary

In conclusion, as the convenience store industry enhances products and services by adding components such as quick-service restaurants and banking, canopy design may evolve into shapes and sizes not found today. The appraiser should be aware of emerging trends and indicate how new designs influence property value.

Fuel Equipment and Canopies

Local and regional fuel equipment suppliers. Fuel equipment suppliers provide information about fuel service equipment and its estimated value. Appraisers should check the Yellow Pages to locate suppliers in their areas. Most fuel equipment suppliers furnish and install fuel service as a package. The package may include USTs, dispensers, electronics, and piping. The canopy may be installed either by the fuel equipment supplier or by the building contractor.

Product manufacturers such as Gilbarco, Wayne, etc.
Gilbarco
www.gilbarco.com

National Institute of Standards and Technology
100 Bureau Drive, Gaithersburg, MD 20899-3460
Petroleum Equipment Institute
P.O. Box 2380, Tulsa, OK 74101-2380

Furnishings, Fixtures, and Equipment Assessment

Non-realty convenience store equipment generally falls into two categories: store equipment and restaurant equipment. Equipment appraisal differs from real estate appraisal, but convenience store appraisers are often asked to provide an opinion of value for non-realty equipment associated with convenience stores. This chapter discusses tangible assets of the convenience store that are not classified as real estate.

Before accepting any assignment, an appraiser should be familiar with the Uniform Standards of Professional Appraisal Practice (USPAP). Appraisers of convenience store equipment should know certain standards in particular. USPAP Standard 1-2(e) requires the appraiser to "identify…any personal property, trade fixtures, or intangible items that are not real property but are included in the appraisal." Standard 1-4(g) requires the appraiser to "analyze the effect on value of any personal property, trade fixtures, or intangible items that are not real property but are included in the appraisal."[1] Standard 7 addresses personal property appraisal development, and Standard 8 addresses personal property appraisal reporting.

Real property appraisers and equipment appraisers define value differently. Real property appraisers typically define value as the market value. However, the

1.   The Appraisal Foundation, *Uniform Standards of Professional Appraisal Practice,* 2003 ed., 16, 19.

definition of value used in equipment appraisal depends on the type of appraisal assignment. Overall, equipment appraisers have five definitions of value. They are

1. Cost of reproduction
2. Fair market value
3. Fair market value in use
4. Orderly liquidation value
5. Forced liquidation value

Descriptions of each type of value follow.

Cost of reproduction. The *cost of reproduction* is a professional opinion of the equipment's cost, expressed in terms of cash in U.S. dollars, F.O.B. (free on board) the manufacturer's plant. It is the current cost of the equipment quoted in current dollars. The cost of reproduction does not include shipping, setup, or installation or any allowance for depreciation.

Fair market value. *Fair market value* is a professional opinion of the estimated most probable price expressed in terms of cash in U.S. dollars. It represents an exchange between a willing buyer and a willing seller, neither of whom is under any compulsion to buy or sell and both of whom are fully aware of the facts, by the effective date of the appraisal report. The term *fair market value* is used when equipment is removed from a property and sold on the open market without duress and with adequate, reasonable, and sufficient exposure time.

Fair market value in use. Like fair market value, *fair market value in use* is a profes- sional opinion of the estimated most probable price expressed in terms of cash in U.S. dollars. It reflects an exchange between a willing buyer and a willing seller, neither of whom is under any compulsion to buy or sell. Both parties are aware of the facts, such as the age and condition of the equipment, as installed for the in- tended use. Fair market value in use differs from fair market value in that it as- sumes that the equipment remains in place. The term *fair market value in use* is used when equipment is included in the property's total assets. It is an appropriate definition when the appraisal is intended to determine the equipment's contribu- tory value to the whole property.

Orderly liquidation value. *Orderly liquidation value* is a professional opinion of the estimated most probable price expressed in terms of cash in U.S. dollars that a piece of equipment could command at a privately negotiated sale that is properly advertised and professionally managed. The seller is obligated to sell over an ex- tended period of time, usually within six to 12 months, as of the effective date of the appraisal report. The equipment is not considered as individual items but as part of a whole marketing package of assets. Any deletions or additions to the total as- sets appraised could change the psychological or monetary appeal needed to achieve the indicated value. All assets should be sold on a piecemeal basis "as is." Purchasers are responsible for the removal of assets at their own risk and expense.

Forced liquidation value. *Forced liquidation value* is a professional opinion of the estimated most probable price expressed in terms of cash in U.S. dollars which could typically be realized at a properly advertised and conducted public auction, held under forced sale conditions and current economic trends, as of the effective date of the appraisal report. The definition of forced liquidation value considers factors such as location, difficulty of removal, physical condition, adaptability, specialization, marketability, physical appearance, and psychological appeal. The ability of the total package of equipment to attract enough prospective buyers to ensure competitive offers also is considered. All assets are to be sold on a piecemeal basis "as is." Buyers must remove assets at their own risk and expense. Any deletions or additions to the total assets appraised could change the psychological or monetary appeal necessary to achieve the value indicated.

Valuing Equipment

Appraising new equipment that will be installed as part of a proposed convenience store is simple. If the proposed convenience store meets the property's highest and best use, the equipment's value can be measured by the owner's cost, which is usually the cost new. Oil companies and restaurant franchises require convenience stores to install specific brands and models of equipment. Equipment costs can easily be estimated from equipment supplier invoices. Between 1990 and 2000, the average cost of merchandise equipment increased by 221%, an average of 29% per year.[2] From 1980 to 2000, the cost increased by 347%, an average annual increase of 21% per year (see Table 6.1 and Figure 6.1).

Equipment can depreciate rapidly when economic conditions change. The appraiser and the client should understand which definition of value is sought. For example, sometimes the contributory value of a national oil company sign may be negligible. For example, the value of a Texaco sign may be zero when the store is being re-branded to Shell.

The economic life of a piece of equipment is shorter than a building's life. Consequently, the value of used equipment more than five years old may be low compared to its cost new.

The value of used equipment may be estimated in a variety of ways. One way to estimate equipment value is to compare equipment sales transactions. Item-by-item comparisons can be made, or contributory value may be estimated on a per- square-foot basis. For example, assume that $75,000 is allocated for the food service equipment in a convenience store in the sale agreement. If the building has 3,000 square feet, the equipment's price could be allocated at $25 per square foot ($75,000 /3,000).

---

2. The percentage increases cited here are not compounded.

Table

6.1	Cost Trends in Equipment per Store

Year	Average Cost	Year	Average Cost
2000	$175,300	1989	$51,700
1999	$135,800	1988	$65,600
1998	$115,100	1987	$64,500
1997	$89,700	1986	$68,300
1996	$102,200	1985	$63,300
1995	$127,500	1984	$61,000
1994	$101,900	1983	$53,600
1993	$81,100	1982	$70,700
1992	$86,800	1981	$51,800
1991	$54,300	1980	$39,200
1990	$54,500		

Figure

6.1	Cost Trends in Equipment

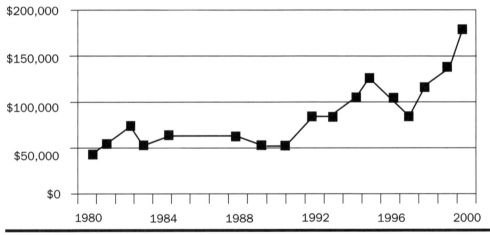

Source: National Association of Convenience Stores

In the case of food service equipment, the unit of comparison may be the value of the equipment per seat. If the convenience store has a seating capacity of 20, the food service equipment can be valued at $3,750 per seat ($75,000/20). The appraiser must remember that sometimes the stated value of equipment is inflated or overexpensed for tax purposes. By allocating a greater portion of the property's sale price to equipment rather than real estate, the buyer is able to deduct a larger depreciation allowance due to the equipment's shorter economic life.

The value of used equipment also may be estimated by using natural cost service publications, such as the one published by Marshall-Swift L.P. Replacement costs for various types of equipment and depreciation tables are provided, but costs from national cost service publications may not reflect local market conditions.

Several equipment suppliers have helpful and informative Web sites that include online photographs, product descriptions, and catalogs of used equipment. Used equipment suppliers are listed at the end of this chapter.

A convenience store appraiser also may ask an experienced equipment appraiser for help in valuing used equipment in preparing the appraisal report. Machinery and equipment appraisers are listed in appraisal, telephone, and online directories.

When it is hard to find a sufficient number of equipment sales transactions the appraiser may use a combination of any of these methods to estimate a piece of used equipment's value. Depreciated book value, a term used in bookkeeping, is an accounting concept and does not reflect the market value definitions above. The appraiser should not assume that the depreciated book value is the market value of the subject property's equipment. If the subject is involved in a sale, the allocation of equipment value in the sale agreement is not sufficient to establish the equipment's market value.

Types of Equipment

Equipment is defined as the assets used in a convenience store operation that are not part of the real estate. Convenience store equipment varies from store to store. Typical convenience store equipment is listed in Figure 6.2. The list, which was provided by an architect, is an actual equipment list for a new Texaco convenience store without a co-branded quick-service restaurant. The list includes gondolas (freestanding merchandise shelving), end caps, a pay phone, and a safe.

Food Service Equipment

Food service equipment is considered separately from other equipment only if the convenience store has branded food service such as a quick-serve restaurant. Food service equipment of nonbranded, in-store food service is usually not extensive and does not need to be considered separately. Figure 6.3 shows how the A&W Company specifies the food service equipment in one of its co-branded QSRs. In this case, the owner-operator had to buy specific brands and models of food service equipment as part of the franchise agreement.

Walk-in coolers must be carefully described in the appraisal. Some walk-in coolers are built in as part of the real estate; others are pre-engineered, modular units that are removable and not considered part of the real estate. Although there may be little difference in the value of a built-in cooler and a modular cooler, the appraiser

6.2 New Equipment List for a Convenience Store

1. CO_2 tank with valve connected to soda machine
2. Drink dispenser with remote tank system
3. Coffee maker
4. Hot chocolate machine
5. Cup dispenser
6. Cash register
7. Telephone board
8. Portable fire extinguisher
9. Vegi prep with sink
10. Ice machine
11. Time recorder
12. Corner cap
13. Bag in box
14. Microwave
15. Fish and game license
16. Popcorn machine
17. Slush puppy
18. Pastry case
19. Hot dog case
20. Gondolas with end caps
21. Two-foot-wide shelving, 72 inches high
22. Espresso machine
23. Pay phone
24. Manager's desk
25. Shelves
26. Under-the-counter safe
27. Lottery machine
28. Receipt machine
29. Credit card machine
30. Condiment tray
31. ATM machine
32. Ice cream machine
33. Three-door freezer
34. Printer
35. Display case

Figure

6.3 | Portion of an A&W Equipment Specification

A&W Restaurants, Inc.
One A&W Drive
Farmington Hills MI 48331
(Phone) 248-699-2000
(Fax)248-553-4643

Date
4/27/99

Page 1

Bill to:
Greg & Chris, Inc.
A& W Restaurant
6200 Highway 95
Fruitland, Id 83619

Ship to:
Greg & Chris, Inc.
A& W Restaurant
6200 Highway 95
Fruitland, Id 83619

Purchase Order No.	Customer Id	Account Executive	Shipping Method	Payment Terms	Required Date	Master Number
	101790				0/00/00	2,782

Quantity Ordered	Quantity Shipped	Quantity BO	Item Number	Description	Site	U of M
	4		600100B	Shelf, 4-Shelf Unit, 24Dx48Lx78H	$157.44	$629.76
	1		60012BA	Sink, Hand w/Soap & Towel Disp AW-CHS-5	$328.90	$328.90
	1		600311A	Faucet, Pre-Rinse Assy Wall Mount w/12" Spout	$213.33	$212.33
	3		600170A	Lever Waste Handle, 2"	$51.13	$153.39
	1		600180A	Mug Washer, Perlick, #PKRB2424	$4,084.40	$4,084.40
	1		600299A	Fryer MJH250 Kit	$9,038.00	$9,038.88
	1		600290A	Fryer 2-Vat, MJH250-CSD		
	1		600292A	Filter, Footprint Frymaster for MJHZ or ZH17C		
	1		600291A	Casters, Frymaster Fryers		
	2		60029BA	Fryer, Fry Vat Cover 21-1/2 x 15" (gas) #8065518		
	1		60029XA	Fryer, Shortening Disposal Unit #SDU50	$413.19	$413.19
	1		600300A	Dormont Kit	$381.05	$381.05
	1		60047EA	Gas Hose 3/4" x 48" w/DBL Swivel (Grill)		
	1		60030BA	Gas Hose, 1" x 48" DBL Swivel (Fryer)		
	2		600310A	Restraining Device for Gas Hose RDC-48		
	1		60032PA	Hood, 69" Non-Compensating w/Prepipe & Shroud	$1,780.00	$1,780.00
	1		60032AA	Ansul System	$1,584.00	$1,584.00
	1		60050A	Freezer, Frigidaire 8-7 Chest w/ Sliding Top	$587.00	$587.00
	2		600360A	Microwave, Panasonic #NE1757	$918.01	$1836.02
	1		600401A	Carmelizer, Bun, Prince Castle #297	$966.90	$966.90
	1		600410A	Landing Shelf, Heated, Watco GRS-24	$267.66	$267.66
	1		600420A	Bun shelf, Wall Mount	$276.00	$276.00
	1		60043LA	Dress Table, 70" Warmer, RH AWOGA129(w/o Warranty)	$5,077.00	$5,077.00
	1		60043LW	Warranty, 5 yr, 1/3 HP (for 70" R&L)	$85.00	$85.00
	1		600460N	Grill, Vulcan 936A Kit	$4,044.70	$4,044.70

should note how a walk-in cooler is classified. Coolers are classified by their square footage, temperature levels, and number of front glass doors. The refrigeration equipment and merchandise loading door for the walk-in cooler should be considered part of the cooler whether the cooler is classified as equipment or part of the real estate. Other refrigerated display cases such as freezer display cases and reach-in coolers should be classified as equipment. The appraiser should ask the following three questions to determine if equipment is personal property or part of the real estate:

1.   Is the item permanently attached to the building or is it moveable?

2. Would the building suffer a loss in function if the item, such as a through-the-wall air-conditioner, were removed?

3. What was the builder's intent when the item was installed?

Carwash Equipment

Carwash equipment is treated separately from store and food service equipment. Although a building shell is considered part of the real estate, carwash equipment is not, regardless of whether it is a wand-type operation, a self-serve operation, or an automatic drive-thru system (see Figure 6.4). Carwashes fall into the following categories:

- Self-service carwash
- Exterior-rollover carwash
- Exterior-only carwash
- Full-service carwash
- Detail shop carwash

Self-Service Carwash. A self-service carwash typically has an open bay–an area where the car drives into the carwash–and a pressure sprayer and foaming brush connected to a large central pump. The sprayer has a coin-operated dialing system so customers can select the service they want such as soaping, rinsing, and waxing. A timer shuts the water off after a certain period of time, and customers must deposit more coins if they want more water.

Exterior-Rollover Carwash. Exterior-rollover carwashes are automated systems. Customers drive their cars into the bay and, once the car is properly positioned, a signal tells customers to stop. The carwash equipment applies soap and rinses the car with each pass. Exterior-rollover systems are common at gas stations. If a customer buys gas, the price of the carwash is often discounted.

Figure 6.4 Interior of a Typical Automated Carwash

Exterior-Only Carwash. The exterior-only carwash system is an automated system that is most popular in the Northeast. Customers drive their cars into the entrance of a long, tunnel-like bay. The front tire, usually on the driver's side, is positioned on a special conveyor belt. When the customer puts the car into neutral, the conveyor belt guides the car through the bay. The car passes by several pieces of equipment, each of which has a specific purpose such as soaping or rinsing.

Full-Service Carwash. A full-service carwash uses the same conveyor belt-based automated system as the exterior-only system. However, in a full-service carwash, employees clean the car's interior and exterior manually, performing services such as drying the car and cleaning the wheels by hand.

Detail Shop Carwash. At a detail shop, attendants wash cars either by hand or using an automated system. They wax, clean, and polish the cars. Dull paint and small scratches can be removed, carpets and seats can be steam-cleaned, chrome can be brightened, and tar can be removed.

Economics of a Carwash

Self-service, wand-type service is the least costly type of carwash. Fully automated carwashes are a major capital investment and are usually only found at stand-alone carwash businesses. In deciding which type of system is best for a particular location, operators and appraisers must consider cost and *throughput*–the number of cars that a carwash can accommodate per hour.

Carwash equipment suppliers estimate that one bay can accommodate 1,000 area residents. Because self-service carwashes can be located in many areas, the cost of the carwash and the equipment's condition are more important to the business than the carwash location.

Exterior-rollover systems are the most common type of carwash systems at convenience stores despite the fact that their prices have soared in recent years. The conveyor belt system used in exterior-only or mini-tunnel carwashes can be purchased for nearly the same price as an exterior-rollover system. A *mini-tunnel system* is usually 30 to 40 feet long. It is called a mini-tunnel because the standard tunnel system is typically 80 feet long or longer. Mini-tunnel systems are popular because most convenience store sites are too small to accommodate standard tunnel systems. Exterior-rollover systems can only accommodate between 12 and 15 cars per hour, whereas mini-tunnel systems can accommodate between 35 and 65 cars per hour.

Touchfree systems are carwashes in which no part of the wash system contacts the car, thus avoiding scratches that may be caused by other types of carwashes. Touchfree systems found in some exterior-rollover systems require expensive chemicals, water heaters, and water softeners. Mini-tunnel systems have a better return on investment than exterior-rollover systems. The operator can maximize the number of cars that are washed during peak hours, and operation costs are considerably lower. Mini-tunnel systems also can use more recycled water than exterior-rollover systems, saving 20% to 30% on water and sewer costs.

The appraiser should discuss carwash volume with the convenience store operator to determine how much traffic the store will experience hourly. Car counts are crucial to the success of a mini-tunnel system. The number of cars that use a carwash is called the *capture rate*, which is expressed as a percentage of the average daily traffic count that passes by the store. According to industry sources, the national average for traffic entering a tunnel system is 0.76%. For example, if the average daily traffic on the street in front of the store is 10,000 vehicles, the subject carwash will wash 76 cars per day. If the subject site has the potential to do a higher volume than 12 to 15 cars per hour, a mini-tunnel system would be appropriate.

Operating expenses for self-service, wand-type carwash systems are about 17% to 20% of gross revenue, and operating expenses for exterior-rollover systems are about 21% to 25% of gross revenue. These estimates do not include debt service.

Following is an industry profile of a carwash. The article can be found in the May 2002 issue of *Professional Carwashing & Detailing* magazine.

Small C-Store Owner Takes a Gamble

An enhanced carwash play by Wal-Mart could nearly spell doom for Dick Skewis, owner of Village Mart in Billings, Mont., an exterior-only carwash, C-store, gas station and lube.

Skewis said Wal-Mart's two superstores and its other smaller stores in that city have had a tremendously negative impact on his business, which slowed to a trickle when Wal-Mart started selling oil changes and gas in his market.

Village Mart began losing customers after Wal-Mart's superstores began selling oil changes for $11.88, nearly half of the $19.95 that Skewis charged. He then offered free carwashes with the oil changes, and customers told him they went to Village Mart only for the deal, because Wal-Mart's oil changes were cheaper.

"We had several hundred customers who were loyal (to Village Mart), but they're not loyal anymore," Skewis said. "They're trained not to be."

And because Wal-Mart is much bigger than Village Mart, whose carwash has 10 employees, Skewis said the retailer gets more attention from oil and gas suppliers.

Business became so scarce for Skewis that he tried for a year and a half to come up with other business ideas to keep his store from failing, such as an ice cream shop, video store, laundromat, arcade, and even a tanning salon.

"We looked at many things, but you don't know what they're going to do next. They want all the business," Skewis said.

Fortunately, a unique twist in Montana law allowed Skewis to create a business Wal-Mart couldn't—a video gambling casino. As a Montana resident, Skewis can get a gambling license. Wal-Mart, based in Arkansas, cannot.

The casino has saved Skewis' business, generating slightly more business than the carwash since the casino opened last September.

Breakeven Analyses

A breakeven analysis is a useful analytical tool for the convenience store appraiser. As more convenience store operators experience declining fuel sales, they will seek other ways of generating profits and carwashes will become more important to a convenience store's income. A *breakeven analysis* shows the minimum sales a convenience store operator will need in order to pay for the added expense of a carwash. A breakeven analysis can be calculated as either the annual number of washes needed to break even or the breakeven cost per wash. Although a breakeven analysis may be criticized for not recognizing the time value of money, the calculations are simple and used widely in the industry to test the feasibility of a proposed carwash operation. Operators use a breakeven analysis to determine when the carwash will begin to generate profits. For example, if the calculated breakeven number is 8,000 washes per year and the subject's carwash completed 9,000 washes that year, there were 1,000 more washes than what was required to satisfy the carwash operator's investment cost. An operator would consider the revenue from the 1,000 washes to be that year's profit.

The breakeven cost per wash helps to determine if the retail price of a carwash is high enough to cover expenses. If the breakeven cost per wash is $3.25 and the convenience store operator is offering special promotional pricing of washes at $3.00, the convenience store operator is actually losing money from the promotion.

Examples of the breakeven number of washes and the breakeven cost per wash are shown below. The breakeven number of washes can be expressed in terms of the total investment cost or in terms of annual costs. Examples of both are provided.

The examples below are based on a subject property with these characteristics:

- $180,000 in total construction costs
- $24,900 in annual fixed costs (mortgage, taxes, insurance)
- Retail price per carwash of $3.50
- $0.50 variable cost per wash (water, detergent, supplies, utilities, etc.)

Breakeven Washes Figured From Total Investment Cost

The breakeven analysis based on total investment cost shows the number of washes that are needed to exceed the total investment in the carwash operation. The analysis is similar to the payback period concept in investment analysis. The breakeven analysis based on total investment cost helps to determine the feasibility of a proposed carwash addition to a convenience store. Although no specific criteria have been established in the industry, a payback period that exceeds seven or eight years is considered too long and the investment in the carwash would be considered unprofitable.

The formula used to determine how many carwashes are needed for a convenience store to break even on the investment in a carwash is:

BEU (breakeven units) = total costs/(price – variable costs per unit)
where   BEU = $180,000/($3.50 – $0.50)
                BEU = $180,000/$3.00
                BEU = 60,000 washes

With no discounting for time, the subject will need to capture 60,000 carwashes to break even. If the convenience store has 10,000 carwashes per year, it will take six years for the convenience store to break even.

Breakeven Washes Figured From Annual Fixed Costs

The breakeven analysis based on annual fixed costs shows how many washes the convenience store operator must provide annually to cover annual fixed expenses such as the mortgage payment, property taxes, and insurance costs. The number of washes calculated here is considered the minimum number of washes a carwash operation must capture to be able to pay expenses. If the carwash operation is performing below the minimum requirement, it is considered unprofitable. If the carwash operation exceeds the minimum number, the carwash is considered to be profitable.

The formula to determine the number of washes a convenience store operator must provide annually to cover fixed expenses is:

BEU (breakeven units) = annual fixed costs/(price – variable costs per unit)

where   BEU = $24,900/($3.50 – $0.50)

BEU = $24,900/$3.00

BEU = 8,300 washes

With no discounting for the time value of money, the subject will require 8,300 wash transactions per year to break even. If the convenience store has less than this amount annually, fixed costs will not be covered and the business will lose money.

Breakeven Cost per Wash

The breakeven cost per wash shows how much the operator must charge for each wash in order to cover expenses. If the retail price for a wash is below the breakeven cost, the operator is losing money. A retail price above the breakeven cost is considered a profit. This breakeven calculation is especially useful for determining whether a promotional pricing program for a carwash is profitable or unprofitable.

Calculating the breakeven cost per wash can also help determine if a trade area is oversupplied with carwash operations. If the market price of carwashes has been driven downward as a result of oversupply in the market, the appraiser can use the breakeven cost per wash calculation to show that carwash operators lose money when the market retail price falls below the breakeven cost per wash.

The formula used to determine the breakeven cost per wash is:

BED (breakeven dollars) = fixed cost per unit/1 – (variable costs per unit/price)

where   BED = $2.50/1 – ($0.50/$3.50)

BED = $2.50/(1 – 0.143)

BED = $2.50/0.857

BED = $2.92

Assume that the subject property has 10,000 carwash transactions annually. It is wrong to figure the breakeven cost per wash as the total of the fixed costs and variable costs. The fixed charge allocation changes with volume; thus, the breakeven cost per wash also changes with volume. In the above example, the difference between the fixed-price variable ($3.00) and the formula solution ($2.92) may not seem significant. However, in a competitive environment where fuel margins are frequently measured in pennies per gallon, it is important to calculate these figures accurately.

Breakeven Income per Year

The breakeven income per year shows the minimum income the carwash operation must generate to pay annual fixed expenses. The breakeven income per year is based on a specific retail price for each wash. Changing the retail price of a wash used in the formula will cause the breakeven income to change as well. As the retail price increases, the breakeven income per year is reduced because the variable expense becomes a smaller percentage of the total price. Because different retail prices can be substituted in the formula, the breakeven income per year calculation may help to establish an optimum retail price.

The formula for determining the breakeven annual income is:

BED (breakeven dollars) = annual fixed costs/1 – (variable costs per unit/price)

where

$$BED = \$24,900/1 - (\$0.50/\$3.50)$$
$$BED = \$24,900/(1 - 0.143)$$
$$BED = \$24,900/0.857$$
$$BED = \$29,055$$

Assume that the subject property has 10,000 carwash transactions per year. The annual breakeven income from the carwash is $29,055. If the arithmetic in the above equation has already been completed, the annual volume of 10,000 washes can simply be multiplied by the breakeven transaction cost of $2.92 to get the same answer.

Summary

Carwashes are among the most commonly encountered operations in convenience store appraisal. Typically, the convenience store operator constructs the carwash building and the carwash equipment is installed as a separate and complete package from the manufacturer or wholesaler. Although the carwash building is usually considered part of the real estate, the appraisal report should clearly state whether the carwash equipment, such as conveyor belts, brushes, spray mechanisms, and dryers, is also considered part of the real estate. Either classification is acceptable and the classification does not affect the value of the carwash equipment. The next chapter will explore how the appraiser analyzes the value of a carwash operation.

Merchandise Equipment

Used Store Fixtures
Bland Enterprises Inc.
www.blandent.com

Used Store Fixtures and Decor
United American Companies
www.the-showcase.com

Used Store Fixtures and Equipment
National Retail Equipment Liquidators Inc.
www.nrel.com

Food & Beverage Freezers and Coolers
Used Machinery and Equipment
www.ume.cgi.exepc.com

Used Restaurant Equipment
Restaurant Equipment World
www.restaurantequipment.net

Car Wash Industry Information
The Car Wash Appraisal Handbook published by Crowe Enterprises, 1997

3B Industries
2 Industrial Park
P.O. Box 37
Comanche, OK 73529
(580) 439-8876
www.3bindustries.com

Explanation of How Different Car Washes Work
www.howstuffworks.com
Go to car washes from main page.

Industry Overview and Trends
www.carwsh.com

Cleaning Management Institute
www.cmiproducts.com
Surveys on self-service carwashes, including operating data for the industry

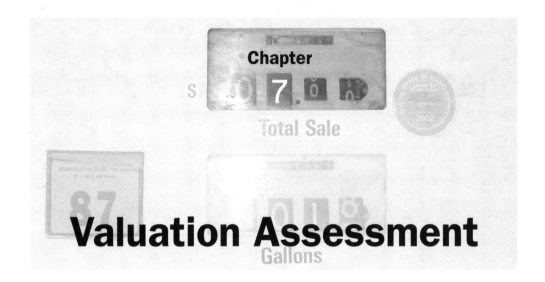

Valuation Assessment

Convenience stores and retail fuel properties are special-purpose properties. However, like any property, a convenience store's market value is determined by supply and demand. As the earlier chapters in this book have shown, many factors impact the supply of and demand for convenience stores. In assessing supply and demand, the appraiser must consider industry trends, the economic characteristics of the local trade area, the suitability of the subject site and building, and the condition and functionality of the fuel service and equipment. All of these factors contribute to a convenience store's market value.

Chapter 7 begins with a discussion of the unique aspects of appraising convenience stores and retail fuel properties. It goes on to discuss the three approaches to value and explains how they apply to convenience store properties.

Not every convenience store is appraised the same way. Each assignment involves unique issues. To properly appraise a convenience store, an appraiser must exercise good judgment. This chapter emphasizes how important it is for the appraiser to assess the state of the convenience store industry, the local market, and the design and functionality of the subject improvements.

Outline of a Convenience Store Appraisal Report

A convenience store appraisal report has sections not found in reports of appraisals of other property types. To make their jobs easier, appraisers should develop outlines of their reports before they begin to write them. One suggested outline format is shown in Figure 7.1.

Figure

7.1 **Example of an Appraisal Outline Format**

I. Executive summary

II. Identification of the property

    A. Appraisal exclusions

III. Legal description

IV. Sales history

V. Scope of work

VI. Competency rule

VII. Purpose, date, and intended user of the appraisal

VIII. Definition of market value

IX. The convenience store industry

    A. Current trends

    B. Industry sales trends

    C. Convenience store growth

    D. Fuel sales statistics

    E. Merchandise sales statistics

    F. Food service trends

    G. Store operations

    H. Current convenience store industry trends in the state

    I. Projected industry growth trends for the state

X. Local data

    A. Employment trends

    B. Per capita personal income

    C. Population trends

XI. Location quotient analysis

XII. Immediate area description

    A. Neighborhood boundaries

    B. Description of subject neighborhood

    C. Traffic patterns

    D. Competitive convenience stores

    E. Assessment of the competition

XIII. Description of the subject property

    A. Site description

Figure

7.1 | **Example of an Appraisal Outline Format** (*continued*)

    B. Physical measurements

    C. Possible environmental hazards

    D. Apparent easements

    E. Off-site improvements

XIV.   Zoning

XV.   Current assessment and property taxes

XVI.   Improvement description

    A. Building

    B. Fuel service

    C. Outside improvements

    D. Estimated effective age and remaining economic life

        1. Physical deterioration

        2. Functional utility

XVII.   Highest and best use

    A. Highest and best use as though vacant

    B. Highest and best use as improved

XVIII. Appraisal methods

XIX.   Opinion of site value

XX.   Cost approach

XXI.   Sales comparison approach

XXII.   Income capitalization approach

XXIII. Final reconciliation

General Considerations in Estimating Convenience Store Value

All three traditional valuation approaches can be applied to convenience stores. Although the cost approach plays an important role in the valuation of new convenience stores, it is not helpful in the appraisal of a store that is more than a few years old. However, conclusions developed in the cost approach can play an important role in developing the sales comparison and income capitalization approaches.

The sales comparison and income capitalization approaches as they apply to convenience stores are the primary focus of this chapter. Because convenience store appraisals are unique and challenging, the appraiser should process both the sales comparison and income capitalization approaches and never rely solely on one approach to value.

When appraising an existing convenience store that has been in business for a few years, the cost approach will be least useful; the sales comparison approach will be moderately useful; and the income capitalization approach will be most useful. In preparing a convenience store appraisal, the appraiser should take the time to develop a sound income capitalization approach.

Obtaining Sales and Operating Data

Sales and operating data is essential in appraising convenience store property. Convenience stores are specialized properties, and few useful market data sources are available to a convenience store appraiser. However, a few sources are helpful for convenience store appraisers who want to learn how to obtain sales and operating data.

To analyze the convenience store market effectively, the appraiser must know more details about comparable sale properties than merely the sale price, date of sale, and physical characteristics. The appraiser also must know the operating characteristics of the comparable sales properties. Operating data includes the annual gallonage, gross fuel and in-store sales, and product margins. In this respect, the local assessor's office will be less than useful. An assessor's office rarely has a separate category for convenience stores, especially when the property's operating data was recorded by an ad valorem tax appraiser.

Sources of Sales Data

Sales data sources the appraiser will find useful include

1. Specialized real estate brokers
2. Convenience store owners
3. Proprietary databases

Specialized Real Estate Brokers

Multiple listing services in small towns typically do not include adequate numbers of convenience store sales. Convenience stores are seldom sold through the local real estate agents that constitute the membership of the multiple listing services. When multiple listing services consolidate, however, their broader geographic coverage makes it easier for appraisers to track convenience store sales through MLS databanks. When a convenience store is sold, it is either sold directly to a knowledgeable buyer or listed with a prominent commercial brokerage firm that specializes in convenience stores. The convenience store appraiser should seek out local brokers who have a history of marketing convenience stores. Usually the list of potential real estate brokers will be limited to those handling commercial real estate. Only a few brokers will have extensive experience with convenience stores. Looking at copies of past marketing advertisements that include convenience store listings is a good way to gauge if a particular brokerage has experience with convenience stores.

Convenience Store Owners

Convenience store owners are usually familiar with their competitors because they need to know the market. The appraiser can obtain information about potential sales from local convenience store operators. Simply asking if the owner knows of any convenience store sales that have occurred within the last couple of years will often turn up a few leads. Typically convenience store owners are only familiar with their direct competitors and are unlikely to know of sales outside their own competitive markets.

Proprietary Databases

Although they were not widely available until recently, *proprietary databases* are becoming an increasingly important and cost-effective tool for obtaining data on specialized property types such as convenience stores. Proprietary databases are specifically targeted to real estate appraisers and people who use individual property sales data. Proprietary databases charge a fee for each property sale the user selects. Once selected, the sales information is transmitted via the Internet, a fax machine, or the conventional mail system. Sale properties may be identified by geographic area, property type, or both.

Proprietary databases are easy to use and access. High-quality digital photographs are usually included in the package or are available for an additional fee. Proprietary sales databases are a new technological development and the appraiser must exercise due diligence when using them. Appropriate disclosures with regard to the extent that the appraiser has verified the information and whether or not the appraiser has inspected the comparable sales should be clearly communicated to the client in the appraisal report.

Examples of convenience store sales data available from major private databases are shown on the following pages. Presently, the extent of comparable sales data is limited. Typically, private databases include only the sale price, the sale date, and rudimentary physical details of the sale property. Because it is essential for the appraiser to know historical operating data such as total gross sales and fuel gallonage, proprietary databases usually provide only a sale lead or a place for the appraiser to begin. The appraiser should be prepared to gather additional information from one of the parties to the transaction. The sale will be most useful to the appraiser once specific details can be confirmed and used in the appraisal analysis.

Early in the development of proprietary databases the number of sales in a particular market may be limited and the quality of the operating data may be poor. The appraiser will probably not be able to acquire information about all convenience store sales within a given area because sales that are input into proprietary databases are not from every source in the region. Proprietary databases usually obtain comparable sales data from a few appraisers or brokers in the particular geographic area. The relatively small number of participating suppliers of information limits the number of sales that are available in proprietary databases. In their current form, proprietary databases should be considered a supplemental source in the search for comparable sales data.

Internet capabilities and dot com companies are changing rapidly. Some important online sources of convenience store sales are LoopNet, BizComps, and CoStar Comps.

LoopNet. LoopNet is affiliated with the Appraisal Institute and includes four search options. The search options allow appraisers to access the Appraisal Institute commercial database, the AppraiserLoop private company database, LoopNet sale listings, LoopNet lease listings, the NRB Shopping Center database, and the IDM assessor and recorder database.

The Appraisal Institute commercial database contains more than 100 listings of convenience store sales in the United States. The data posted pertains mostly to the East and Midwest. Little coverage is given to Western states.

LoopNet is a work in progress. Many convenience store sales records on the site are incomplete, providing little more than an address, sale price, sale date, building size, and site size. However, LoopNet can direct the appraiser to valuable leads.

Navigating LoopNet is easy. Many of the features are integrated, which makes it efficient to use the material provided. For example, once the size of the market area has been selected, say one-quarter mile, one-half mile, and one mile from the property, the traffic count and demographic summary can be printed with one click of the mouse. LoopNet members can get a basic year subscription for free, although listings are limited. LoopNet also offers a premium membership for $39.95 per month. A premium membership includes maximum listing exposure, unrestricted searching access, and more. To access LoopNet online, go to *www.loopnet.com*. An example of a LoopNet commercial real estate listing is shown in Figure 7.2.

BizComps. Designed and developed for business appraisers rather than real estate appraisers, BizComps is a comprehensive source of thousands of commercial business sales. Sorting is generally keyed to the SIC Code or NAICS code. For convenience stores, these codes are 5411 and 44511, respectively.

BizComps includes more than 300 convenience store sales dating back to 1995. A sample transaction report is shown in Figure 7.3. Reported data does not include the individual property address or information about the property's physical characteristics. BizComps is a valuable appraisal source because the data can be used to help develop market-derived rates of return based on seller cash flow to gross sales, sale price to gross sales, and sale price to seller cash flows. It is the most comprehensive source of data on economic returns. Increasingly, courts are requiring market-based data to support the capitalization rates and rates of return used in appraisal reports.

For one-time access to the data, the appraiser pays $99 to access all the information contained in the sale database. The information includes a broad classification of sale properties based on the first two digits of the SIC code classification.

Figure
7.2   Sample of A LoopNet Commercial Real Estate Listing

Offering Summary

Listing status:	Sold
Property ID:	13328925
Property type:	Retail-commercial
Subtype:	Service station/gas station
Address:	2275 W. Santa Clara Drive
	Santa Clara, UT 84765
	United States
County:	Washington

Price:	$820,000			
Down payment:	N/A			
Sq. ft.:	1,500			
Lot size:	0.50 acr.			
Use type:	Business			
Investment:	Cap rate:	N/A	Proforma	
Factors:	Cash-on-cash:	N/A	Proforma	
	Price/sq. ft.:	$546.67		
	Built:	N/A		
Last Verified:	7 Aug 2002			

Property Description

Inventory estimated at an additional $25,000. C-store with restaurant building, convenience store, gas pumps, and carwash. 12 storage units plus office/warehouse available for an additional $865,000.

Location Description

Santa Clara

Contact Information

NAI Utah Commercial Real Estate	Mark Walter	Phone: 435-628-1606
Southern Region		

13328925 11/29/2001

Figure

7.3 **Sample of BizComps• Convenience Store Sales Data**

BIZCOMPS® Transaction Report Prepared: 11/6/02 1:24:07 PM (PST) N/A=Not Available

Transaction Details

Business description	Convenience Store
SIC	5411 Grocery Stores
NAICS	44512 Convenience Stores
Location	El Cajon, CA
Number of employees	N/A

Transaction Data

Sale date	11/30/93
Days on market	N/A
Ask price (000)	$250.00
Sale price (000)	$200.00
Percent down	40.0%
Terms on outstanding consideration	4 Years

Income Data ($000's)		**Asset Data ($000's)**	
Annual gross sales	$360.00	Inventory value	$45.00
Franchise royalty	N/A	Furniture, fixtures, and equipment	$30.00
SDCF	$60.00	Value of real estate	N/A

Operating Ratios		**Valuation Multiples**	
SDCF/annual gross sales	0.167	Sale price/Annual gross sales	0.556
Rent/annual gross sales	8.3%	Sale price/SDCF	3.333

For example, the SIC classification for convenience stores falls under retail sales businesses, which also includes grocery stores.

To access BizComps online, go to *www.bvmarketdata.com* for the home page of Business Valuation Resources. Several other related databases are shown on the Web site and BizComps can be accessed from their home pages as well.

CoStar Comps. More than 650,000 property sales are included in the CoStar Comps database. Appraisers can access data by property type, region, and sale price. CoStar Comps lists more than 300 convenience store sales and provides comprehensive information on individual sales. Once purchased, the data is transmitted either online or by fax in less than an hour. Prices range from $35 to $58, depending on the sale's location and the complexity of the data. A $35 daily access fee is charged for searches. No subscription is required. For an additional fee of $10 each, high-quality digital photographs will be e-mailed to the appraiser.

Online proprietary databases are still in their infancy but they are already an important source for obtaining sales information on specialized property types such as convenience stores. However, appraisers should be cautious. Much of the data input is developed by brokers, mortgage lenders, and business appraisers–not real estate appraisers.

Brokers, mortgage lenders, and business appraisers speak a slightly different language than real estate appraisers. For example, the terms *operating expenses* and *net operating income* are defined differently in various proprietary databases. Often it is difficult for the appraiser to know how the dollar amounts for net income listed for the sale property were calculated. Without uniform definitions it is difficult for the appraiser to use the financial measures supplied by these data sources. The appraiser should also be aware that the convenience store industry has its own way of defining revenue and operating expenses. None of the generic data sheets for sales included in these databases lend themselves to analyzing convenience stores, which are a specialized type of income-producing property.

Obtaining Information Through Interviews

To obtain detailed information about sale transactions, which is often not available from any other source, an appraiser must interview property buyers and sellers. In an interview with a convenience store owner-operator, the appraiser's knowledge of the industry and communication skills are important. The appraiser should be prepared to listen and ask key questions to obtain the necessary information about the sale.

The convenience store appraiser must obtain more information than the property's sale price. The appraiser must know how the property was operating at the time of sale, including

- The number of gallons (gallonage) typically sold in the year of sale
- The amount of in-store sales
- The age of the fuel service
- Whether pay-at-the-pump technology was installed at the time of sale
- Whether equipment value and business value were included in the sale price

The appraiser should advise the person being interviewed that the information will not be made available to the general public. Below are techniques to use when interviewing the buyer or seller of a convenience store or retail fuel property. The appraiser should

1. Ask the buyer and seller about their motivations. Why did the seller sell the property? Was it because of health problems? Was the store a poor performer? The appraiser should specifically ask if any environmental or contamination issues were present at the time of sale.

2. Inquire about the number of competing properties present at the time of sale and what the business environment was at the time. It may have changed. The seller may have sold just prior to the construction of a hypermarket fuel site a block away. This would be important information for the appraiser to know.

3. Ask how many gallons of fuel (gallonage) were sold in the year of sale. It is more important to know the gallonage in the year of sale than the store's current gallonage. It is also important to know what would have been typical in the year of sale. The appraiser may have to urge the person being interviewed to recall if road construction or another outside influence during the year of sale could have skewed the gallonage. The appraiser should also ask about gallonage trends. Was gallonage rising, declining, or flat at the time of sale?

4. Determine the fuel margin at the time of sale. It is usually better to express this as a percentage of gross fuel sales, rather than cents per gallon. Often, the percentage and cents per gallon figures will be close. To avoid confusion, the appraiser should ask the person being interviewed which number is being supplied. For example, if the person being interviewed simply states that the fuel margin was nine, the appraiser does not know if that means $0.09 per gallon or 9% of gross fuel sales. Either figure could be reasonable, but the difference could be significant.

    Many stores are either chain stores or part of pools that set up specialized marketing arrangements with various suppliers. This can result in sizeable rebates to the convenience store operator. For example, rebates may be offered to the convenience store operator if only one type of bread or milk is sold in the store. National oil companies frequently offer the operator rebates of $0.01 to $0.04 per gallon on their brand of gasoline when the market is especially competitive. The appraiser must know if such rebates exist, how much income is produced, and what is the source of the income. The appraiser must then determine if the income affects the property's value.

5. Ask about all annual sales other than fuel sales, i.e., in-store sales. In-store sales include merchandise, food service, and other categories such as carwash sales. The appraiser must know the sales in each of these categories because the gross margin is different for each. Although national and regional average margins for each of these categories can be obtained from third-party sources such as the National Association of Convenience Stores and state-of-the-industry reports, the interview is a good time to ask about the store's performance. As a last resort, published retail prices and margin reports are available online at *www.api.org/consumers/gaspricecharts.htm* and at *www.opisnet.com.*

6. Ask about the property's physical condition at the time of sale. The property's condition may have been different than it appears at the time of the interview. The appraiser should specifically ask about the fuel service because technology is changing so rapidly that the fuel service may be modified every couple of years. Was pay-

at-the-pump service available at the time of sale? What was the condition of the underground fuel tanks? Had any recent upgrades been made to the building?

7. Ask the person being interviewed if the price was fair, too high, or too low. Often buyers or sellers will give reasons for their answers and the additional information is helpful for the appraiser.

A sale interview checklist is shown in Figure 7.4. If the sale properties are located in the same competitive market, the current posted fuel price should also be

Figure

7.4 Sale Interview Checklist

Neighborhood	Operations
Competitive properties within one mile	Annual gallonage
Neighborhood age	Merchandise sales
Neighborhood trend	**Food Service Sales**
Site	Carwash sales
Frontage	Other
Depth	Alcohol sales
Traffic count	Fuel margin
Customers per day	Merchandise margin
Traffic capture rate	Food service margin
Access rating	Carwash margin
Paved out area	Other average margin
Building	**Currently Posted Fuel Sales**
Size	Regular
Age	Blend
Public restrooms	Premium
Condition	Diesel
Fuel Service	**Sale Price**
Dispensers	Sale date
Canopy	Portion to real estate
USTs	Portion to FF&E
Food Service	Portion to inventory
Branded	Portion to business value
Size	Financing
Overall Ratings	Comments about sale price
Condition	**Person Interviewed**
Quality	**Date**
Cleanliness	
Competitiveness	

recorded. The information in the sale interview checklist is easily transferred to the competitive analysis section of the appraisal. The appraiser should photograph all competitive and sale properties. Several photographs of the sales and competitive properties taken from different angles can be produced at a minimal cost.

Real Property, Personal Property, and Business Value

Convenience stores are businesses. As such, their value is derived from several sources. The appraiser should explain to all parties involved in the appraisal how the value estimate is allocated to the various constituent parts. Standard Rule 1-2 (e)[1] requires the appraiser to distinguish real property from non-realty in developing a real property appraisal. A convenience store consists of tangible and intangible assets, as shown in Figure 7.5.

Figure

7.5 | **Tangible and Intangible Assets of a Convenience Store**

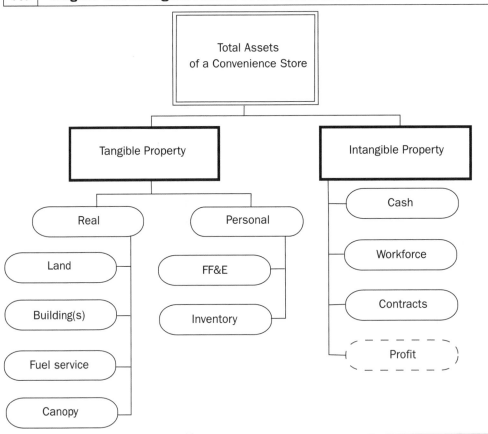

---

1. The Appraisal Foundation, *Uniform Standards of Professional Appraisal Practice,* 2003 ed. (Washington, DC: The Appraisal Foundation, 2003), 16.

Tangible and Intangible Assets

Tangible assets can be classified as real property, personal property, or trade fixtures. *Intangible assets* are assets of the business that are not tangible real property nor tangible personal property. Components of tangible and intangible assets are shown in Table 7.1.

Table 7.1 | **Components of Tangible and Intangible Assets**

Tangible Assets	Classification
Site	Real property
Building	Real property
Fuel service and canopy	Real property or trade fixtures
Furniture, fixtures, and equipment	Trade fixtures or personal property
Inventory	Personal property
Intangible Assets	**Classification**
Cash	Non-real property
Franchises and licenses	Non-real property
Goodwill	Non-real property
Skilled workforce	Non-real property
Other	Non-real property

The property's site and building components are universally recognized as real property assets. Disagreement can arise as to how the fuel service is classified. Fuel service includes underground storage tanks, dispensers, and canopies. Convenience store appraisers usually classify the fuel service as part of the real property. However, whether the fuel service is classified as real property or personal property makes little difference in the valuation. The contributory value of the fuel service should be the same under either classification. The appraiser must be consistent in how the fuel service is classified for the subject property and the comparable sales.

Consider the two examples shown in Table 7.2. Assume that the building has 2,500 square feet. Which price per square foot should the appraiser apply to the subject property? It depends on how the appraiser classifies the subject's fuel service. If the subject's fuel service is not considered part of the real estate, it would be inappropriate to base the subject's value on the higher indication of $240 per square foot.

Twenty years ago, it was common for the petroleum supplier to own the fuel dispensers, canopy, and signage and lease them to the fuel retailer. Under those conditions, it was convenient and common to think of the fuel service as trade

Table

7.2	**Classification of Fuel Service**			

Sale with Fuel Service Included		Sale with Fuel Service Not Included	
Site	$100,000	Site	$100,000
Building	$250,000	Building	$250,000
Fuel service	$250,000		
Total	$600,000	Total	$350,000
Price/sq. ft.	$240	Price/sq. ft.	$140

fixtures and not part of the real property. Although no physical change has taken place, today it is more common for the convenience store operator to own the dispensers, canopy, and signage and for the fuel service to be considered part of the real property. The classification does not affect the value opinion of these components. However, the appraiser and client should understand what is included in the appraisal assignment and how the assets are classified. The convenience store appraisal report should state the classifications clearly.

Many real estate appraisers are unfamiliar with business valuation, which is a separate appraisal discipline. However, it is critical for the convenience store appraiser to recognize that the value of a convenience store may include values other than that of the real property. Some fundamental concepts of business appraisal must be recognized. First, convenience stores operate as income-producing entities and are bought and sold as such. Convenience store income is generated by the tangible and intangible assets. Second, the economic return to the tangible assets, such as the site, building, fuel service, and equipment, is received first. Business value economic theory states that the income produced by a convenience store must first be applied to the investment requirements of tangible assets such as the site, building, fuel service, equipment, and inventory. [2]

Intangible assets such as goodwill only have value if excess earnings exist over and above the required investment return on the tangible assets. The appraiser should not assume that goodwill exists in every case. Frequently, small single-store operations will not have any excess earnings and, consequently, no goodwill value. If the appraisal assignment includes a chain or corporate ownership of several stores, the real estate appraiser is advised to obtain the services of a qualified business appraiser to assist in developing the appraisal. For example, a chain of several stores may realize operating cost savings because general and administrative expenses are spread over several stores. Economies of scale such as this may

2. This concept is the basis for Revenue Ruling 68-609, published by the Internal Revenue Service, which discusses the valuation of intangible assets. For an authoritative statement regarding the priority of the economic return to tangible assets, see Jay E. Fishman, MBA, ASA, CBA, and Shannon P. Pratt, DBA, FASA, CFA, *Guide to Business Valuations*, 12th ed. (Fort Worth: Practitioners Publishing Company, 2002), 7-28.

create a cost advantage that a single-store operation does not enjoy. A trained and assembled workforce is an intangible asset that has economic value.

Because convenience stores frequently sell as going concerns and often must be analyzed as going-concern entities that include tangible and intangible assets, it is highly recommended that convenience store appraisers attend the Appraisal Institute's Course 800, Separating Real and Personal Property from Intangible Business Assets. Much of the procedure and theory in the following valuation sections is based on this course.

Cost Approach

Applying the cost approach to convenience stores is similar to applying the cost approach to other property types. Estimating the site value and replacement cost of the improvements in the cost approach will be useful in allocating the tangible assets in the sales comparison and income capitalization approaches. With few exceptions, the site value establishes the minimum threshold of value for the tangible assets, while the replacement cost of the improvements plus the site value establishes an upper limit of value for the tangible assets.

The cost approach does not include consideration of the value of intangible assets such as capitalized economic profit or franchises, and developing estimates of depreciation is often difficult. Types of physical deterioration, functional obsolescence, and external obsolescence unique to convenience stores are described below.

Physical Deterioration in Convenience Stores

Convenience stores receive a great deal of daily customer traffic because the stores typically sell high-turnover items such as milk and bread and are open longer than most other types of retail businesses. The high customer traffic causes the floor coverings, restroom fixtures, and other features to wear out quickly. The automatic doors and asphalt paving in the forecourt may also deteriorate more quickly than those elements in other retail stores. On the other hand, the building foundation, exterior shell, and roof are similar to other types of commercial construction and usually do not experience any abnormal deterioration. The fuel service, even when it is classified as part of the real property, will have an economic life that is shorter than that of the building.

Functional Obsolescence

The convenience store industry is intensely competitive. Old formats and business models for store operation are continually being replaced with new ideas. To remain competitive, each store must modernize and upgrade frequently. A 10-year-old convenience store can be physically adequate but functionally obsolete when new design standards dominate the market. For example, some early stores were too small to accommodate in-store food service, which could be a form of functional obsolescence.

Rapid changes in technology cause older technologies to become obsolete very quickly. This is particularly true for the electronics associated with fuel service. Several new, noncash customer payment systems are now being tested. The payment system that emerges as dominant will become the design standard for fuel dispensers in the future.

External Obsolescence

The competition for retail fuel sales posed by mass retailers such as Wal-Mart will undoubtedly continue to diminish the value of the fuel service facilities of other convenience stores. A modern and functional fuel service can be worthless in a market where a mass retailer has undercut the fuel sales of competing convenience stores. Already, this market channel displacement appears to be a long-term trend that will forever change the way customers buy gasoline.

Sales Comparison Approach

Although application of the sales comparison approach to convenience stores is similar to its application to other property types, a few notable characteristics of convenience store properties should be considered. The convenience store market is dominated by national and regional owner-operators. Because stores often sell as a group or part of a chain, it may be difficult to find sales of individual stores. Further complicating the analysis, the convenience store market can be divided into two groups. The first group consists of new stores with pay-at-the-pump technology and branded food service. These stores comprise the most expensive stores in the market today. The second group consists of old stores that have outdated designs and technology. These stores are having trouble competing in a highly competitive industry. Old stores are simply worth less than new stores and it is difficult to compare and adjust the price of an old store to a new one.

Many old convenience stores are located in prime traffic areas. Rather than equip old stores with new technology and designs, the improvements are often torn down. The new owner-operator finds the most value in the site itself.

When stores do sell, some type of seller motivation is usually involved. The store is either unprofitable or difficult to manage. Operators simply do not sell profitable stores that are easy to manage. Consequently, stores that are placed on the market have problems. The new buyer sees an opportunity that may be realized—usually through significant capital reinvestment after the sale. To the buyer, the total acquisition cost is the purchase price plus the capital reinvestment. Usually the buyer's pro forma operating statement is based on the assumption that capital improvements will be made and the property is purchased based on an operating scenario that includes the additional investment.

Because the Uniform Standards of Professional Appraisal Practice require (depending on the intended use and user) separate real property value estimates for tangible and intangible assets that are not real property, the appraiser must segregate the sale price of each comparable sale into the various components of tangible and intangible assets, as shown in Table 7.3.[3] The most effective and efficient way to make price allocations is to ask the parties to the transaction how they made the allocations.

Table 7.3 **Allocations of Tangible and Intangible Assets**

Tangible Assets	Classification
Site and building	Real property
Fuel service and canopy	Real property or trade fixtures
Furniture, fixtures, and equipment	Trade fixtures or personal property
Inventory	Personal property
Intangible Assets	**Classification**
Franchises and licenses	Non-real property
Goodwill	Non-real property
Other	Non-real property

Comparable Sale Data Sheet

The allocation of the sale price is entered on a comparable sale data sheet. Because convenience stores are special-use properties, a customized form can be developed specifically to analyze the price and operating data of a convenience store sale property. An example of a customized form is shown in Figure 7.6. The form is six pages long. For simplicity, the intangible assets have been grouped under the heading "total intangible assets." Some of these pages show operating data, which will be discussed further in the income capitalization approach. The form is set up using a spreadsheet program and once the appraiser makes the data entries, the calculations are performed automatically.

After making the appropriate deductions for non-realty furniture, fixtures, and equipment, inventory, and any intangibles, the appraiser is ready to analyze the prices paid for the real estate. Units of comparison include physical and economic units. Explanations of their application follow.

Physical Units of Comparison

The real property price and price per square foot of building area units of comparison can be applied to convenience stores just as they are applied to other property types

3. *Uniform Standards of Professional Appraisal Practice*, Standard Rule 1-4g.

Figure

| 7.6 | **Confidential Market Data** |

Comparable Sale 11
Series No. 1
Index No. CS-8011

The information contained in these pages has been acquired under conditions in which it was agreed that the data would remain confidential. This data may not be disseminated to third parties. Breech of contract legal penalties will apply for violations.

Name	Quick-stop Chevron station
Address	Fifth and Cedar
	Sandpoint, Idaho
Sale price	$1,000,000
Sale date	February 1997
Terms of sale	Typical
Cash equivalent price	$1,000,000
Non-realty included	$10,000
FF&E included	$30,000
Business value included	$50,000
Residual to real estate	$910,000

Quantitative Measures:

Building

Building size	3,024 sq. ft.
Estimated effective age	3 yrs.
Condition of building	Good
Type of construction	Block/flat

Sample Comparable Sale page 1

Figure

7.6 | **Confidential Market Data (*continued*)**

	Comparable Sale 11 Series No. 1 Index No. CS-8011
Quantitative Measures (*continued*):	
Fuel service	
Estimated annual gallonage	1,000,000
Fueling positions	8
Dispensers	(4) Six-hose
Canopy	Steel 40 × 60
Pay at pump	Yes
Food service	
Type	QSR
Size	750 sq. ft.
Branded food service	Yes
Indoor seating	30
Carwash	
Type	Exterior-rollover
Age	3 yrs.
Washes per year	12,000
Other improvements	None
Site	
Site size	142 × 150
Location	Downtown
Neighboring uses	Downtown commercial
Traffic count	20,000
Parking	Adequate/off-street
Excess marketable land	None
Qualitative Measures:	
Quality of management	Average
Quality of property maintenance	Average
Condition of exterior	Good
Condition of interior	Good
Quality of improvements	Good

Sample Comparable Sale page 2

Figure

| 7.6 | **Confidential Market Data (*continued*)** |

Comparable Sale 11

Series No. 1

Index No. CS-8011

Access and visibility	Good/good
Quality of neighborhood	Good
Price trend in neighborhood	Upward
Time on market (months)	Less than 24 months
Highest and best use	Fuel sales
	Convenience store
	Retail store
Verification:	Broker: High Mountain Realty

Additional comments:

This is a new petroleum-marketing convenience store located in downtown Sandpoint at a busy commercial intersection. U.S. Highway 95 passes in front of the property. This building and the fuel service were built just before the sale. The building is current with the design standards of national oil chains. The co-branded QSR has a drive-up window and carries the Taco Bell brand. The fuel service includes the newest technology under an illuminated canopy.

Reconstructed Operating Statement

Estimated gallons per year	1,000,000
Average price per gallon	$1.090
Fuel dollars	$1,090,000
Merchandise (in-store) sales	$500,000
Food service/other	$175,000
Carwash	$40,000
Other	$0
Total sales	$1,805,000

Less cost of goods sold:

Fuel	88%	$959,200
Merchandise	68%	$340,000
Food service	35%	$61,250
Carwash	20%	$8,000
Other		$0
Shrink	1.20%	$21,660
Gross profit margin	23%	$414,890

Sample Comparable Sale page 3

Figure

| 7.6 | **Confidential Market Data (*continued*)** |

Comparable Sale 11

Series No. 1

Index No. CS-8011

Reconstructed Operating Statement (*continued*)

Less operating expenses:

Labor costs	7.00%	$26,350
Liability insurance	0.10%	$1,805
Royalty fees	0.10%	$1,805
Supplies	0.59%	$10,650
Advertising	0.30%	$5,415
Utilities	1.00%	$18,050
Motor fuel drive-offs	0.10%	$1,805
Cash short/over	0.10%	$1,805
Other	1.20%	$21,660
Subtotal	10.49%	$189,345
EBIDTA	12.50%	$225,545

EBIDTA is earnings before interest, depreciation, taxes, and amortization

Operating Profile Summary

Gross sales	100%	$1,805,000
Cost of goods sold	76%	$1,368,450
Operating expenses/shrink	1.2%	$21,660
Gross profit	23%	$414,890

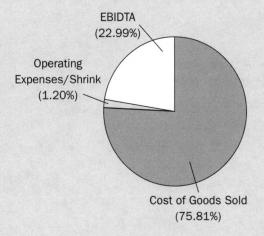

EBIDTA
(22.99%)

Operating
Expenses/Shrink
(1.20%)

Cost of Goods Sold
(75.81%)

Sample Comparable Sale page 4

Figure

7.6 **Confidential Market Data (*continued*)**

		Comparable Sale 11
		Series No. 1
		Index No. CS-8011

Contribution to gross profit

Gross profit	$414,890	
Add: shrink	$21,660	
Total	$436,550	

		Contribution Ratios
Fuel	$130,800	30%
Merchandise	$160,000	37%
Food service	$113,750	26%
Carwash	$32,000	7%
Other		0%
Total		100%

Income Allocation to Real Property

EBIDTA		$225,546	
Income to non-realty	10%	$10,000	$1,000
Income to FF&E	18%	$30,000	$5,400
Income to business value	50%	$50,000	$25,000
Income to real property			$194,146
Less:			
Property taxes	10%	$20,000	
Maintenance and repairs	20%	$38,829	
Reserves for replacement	10%	$19,415	
		$78,244	

Net operating income to real property $115,902

Market-derived units of comparison:

Whole property price	$1,000,000
Non-realty price paid	$10,000
FF&E price paid	$30,000
Business value price paid	$50,000
Real estate price paid	$910,000
Price per square foot of building area	$300.93

Sample Comparable Sale page 5

Figure

| **7.6** | **Confidential Market Data** (*continued*) |

Comparable Sale 11

Series No. 1

Index No. CS-8011

Market-derived units of comparison (*continued*):

Gross sales per square foot	$596.89
Real estate income per square foot	$64.20
Gross sales multiplier*	0.50
Gross profit multiplier*	2.19
Operating margin	23%
Overall capitalization rate*	12.74%

*Calculated for real property only

Plat Map

and recorded in an adjustment grid. The consistency of the results will be affected by how physically similar the sale properties are to the subject. The store building's various physical components—the fuel service, food service, and carwash—should be treated as separate line item adjustments. Examples of convenience store adjustment categories processed in the sales comparison approach are shown in Table 7.4 using the information from Sample Sale 11. Sale 11 is comparable to the subject in location, site size, store building, and food service. However, adjustments are required for food service and a carwash. Sale 11 has a 750-sq.-ft. quick-service restaurant and an exterior-rollover carwash. The subject has no branded food service and no carwash.

Sale Adjustments. The location adjustment should include consideration of visibility, traffic characteristics, and the location's competitiveness. A high-visibility location with too many competitors may not be as good as a less visible location

Table

7.4	Example of Adjustment Categories—Price per Square Foot Comparison	
Sale price (real property)	N/A	$305.89
Date of sale	N/A	February 1997
Adjustment	N/A	+10%
Condition of sale	N/A	Typical
Adjustment	N/A	0%
Base sale price	N/A	$336.48
Location	Average	Inferior
		+5%
Site	20,000 sq. ft.	21,300 sq. ft.
		0%
Building size	3,000 sq. ft.	3,024 sq. ft.
		0%
Building age/condition	Two years/good	Three years/good
		0%
Fuel service	Good	Good
Includes dispensers and canopy		0%
Food service	None	QSR
		-25%
Carwash	None	Exterior-rollover
		-5%
Other	None	None
		0%
Net adjustments		-25%
Indicated value		$252.36

with less competition. The selected adjustment would reflect a balance of all these factors. Frontage and access can be adjusted for under the site category in addition to the overall site area, shape, and other considerations. The building, fuel service, and carwash are treated as separate entities and can vary in physical attributes. For example, one store could have an old, outdated building with modern, upgraded fuel service and no carwash. A comparison property might have a similar building but older, inferior fuel service and an older carwash. By keeping these components separate, the adjustment process is easier for the appraiser.

Technology and design standards for convenience stores change frequently. The age and condition adjustment for a building can be as much as 50% to 75%. When a limited number of sales makes it necessary for the appraiser to compare an older store to a newer store, the building age and condition adjustment could be 100%.

Convenience stores are bought and sold as income-producing properties. Therefore, the fuel service, food service, and carwash adjustments in the sales comparison approach can logically be valued at their contribution to the store's gross margin. The calculations the appraiser must make are shown in Table 7.5. These contributions to the gross margin can be calculated with a spreadsheet.

Note the wide difference between the proportion of fuel sales to total gross sales (60%) and fuel profits to total gross profits (30%). Operating information should also be developed for the market sales used in the sales comparison approach.

Table 7.5 | Adjustment Calculations for Comparable Sale 11

	Fuel	Merchandise	Food Service	Carwash
Gross dollars	$1,090,000	$500,000	$175,000	$40,000
Gross profit (%)	12%	32%	65%	80%
Gross profit (dollars)	$130,800	$160,000	$113,750	$32,000
Gross Profit Summary				
Fuel	$130,800			
Merchandise	$160,000			
Food service	$113,750			
Carwash	$32,000			
Total	$436,550			

	Contribution to Gross Sales	Contribution to Gross Profit
Fuel	60%	30%
Merchandise	28%	37%
Food service	10%	26%
Carwash	2%	7%

The percentage of gross profit is the fundamental measure of contributory value when analyzing the sale. Fuel service, which includes dispensers, canopies, underground storage tanks, electronics, and piping, generally contributes 20% to 40% to gross margin dollars. The line item adjustment should be based on the perception that the entire fuel service is contributing 20% to 40% of the overall property value. Older mechanical pumps might be worth almost nothing compared to modern, electronic dispensers with pay-at-the-pump technology. However, the category adjustment for fuel service could not exceed 40% because in this example fuel sales contribute no more than 40% to gross profit.

Food service can range from simple dedicated counter space to a 2-in-1 concept. The food service's contribution to gross profit can vary from less than 10% to nearly 50%, depending on the extent of the food service improvements. Similarly, a single-bay, drive-thru carwash rarely constitutes more than 10% of gross margin dollars. Usually the carwash operation's contribution to gross margin is 5% to 10%. Therefore, 5% to 10% is the adjustment range for comparing a property with a carwash to one without a carwash.

Economic Units of Comparison

Economic units of comparison can be applied in the sales comparison approach. However, an analysis using economic units of comparison should be treated as a separate part of the sales comparison approach in addition to the analysis using physical units of comparison. If the appraiser processes the sales comparison approach using only economic units of comparison, the appraisal actually consists of an abbreviated income capitalization approach and a long income capitalization approach. Such an appraisal does not include two different approaches with two different perspectives on the subject's value. Both approaches are an analysis of the income stream. If a mistake is made in quantifying the subject's gross income, the mistake will affect both the sales comparison and income capitalization approaches and the resulting error will not be apparent. Instead, the appraiser will have a false sense of accuracy because both approaches had the same mistake and produced similar value estimates.

The appraiser should apply at least one physical unit of comparison in the sales comparison approach. If an economic unit of comparison is used, the appraiser should consider this analysis a supplemental section in the sales comparison approach. The gross sales multiplier is simply the sale price divided by the annual gross sales. The gross sales multiplier method is not preferred because gross sales can vary greatly depending on the wholesale cost (cost of goods sold) of fuel and in-store items. For example, a gallon of regular gasoline in Oregon averaged $1.41 in September 1997. One year later the same gallon cost $1.12. If the subject store sells an average of 1.5 million gallons per year, the difference in gross revenue would be $435,000 per year for gasoline alone. A 0.25 difference in the gross sales multiplier could swing the value estimate by as much as $108,750 when, in reality, there was no significant difference in the subject's net income. Similarly, in 1999 the retail price of cigarettes jumped 31% due to higher wholesale costs. The convenience store operator did not earn more, nor did any extra value accrue to the real estate as a result of the increase.

Gross Profit Multiplier. The preferred economic unit of comparison is the gross profit multiplier. The gross profit is the amount of revenue the convenience store operator has after paying the item's wholesale cost but before paying operating expenses. Table 7.6 shows how a sale would be analyzed when using the gross profit multiplier method for both fuel and in-store sales.

Table 7.6	Analyzing a Sale Using the Gross Profit Multiplier Method for Fuel and In-Store Sales	
Fuel	Fuel sales	$2,000,000
	Fuel margin	10%
	Gross fuel profit	$200,000 (A)
In-Store	Merchandise sales	$1,000,000
	Merchandise margin	25%
	Gross merchandise profit	$250,000 (B)
	Food service sales	$500,000
	Food service margin	50%
	Gross food service profit	$250,000 (C)
	Carwash sales	$50,000
	Carwash margin	80%
	Gross carwash profit	$40,000 (D)

A + B + C + D equals the total gross profit, which in this case is $740,000. If the sale price of the property was $1,600,000, the gross profit multiplier would be 2.16, as shown in the calculation below. This multiplier can be based on the price of the whole comparable property or the price of the real estate. The multiplier must be applied to the subject in the same way it was calculated from the sales.

$$\$1,600,000 \text{ sale price} / \$740,000 \text{ gross profit} = 2.16$$

In making this calculation, the appraiser should remember that the margin is different for each classification of revenue. This is how the sale should be analyzed. Although overall margins are occasionally discussed, the industry tracks fuel sales and in-store sales separately and the appraiser must approach them separately.

After a sufficient number of convenience store sales are analyzed, a gross profit multiplier can be applied to the subject's stabilized gross profit. If the subject has a stabilized gross profit of $1,000,000 and the selected gross profit multiplier is 2.8, the estimated value of the subject is $2,800,000.

The gross profit multiplier has an advantage over the gross sales multiplier because all line items above the gross profit line are equalized in comparing the subject and all of the sales. In other words, a sale that has a high fuel margin can be directly compared to a subject that has a low fuel margin without adjustment. A sale that had a high percentage of fuel sales compared to overall sales could be compared to the reverse situation for the subject. A gross profit multiplier analysis performed in this way provides a more consistent and accurate value estimate for the subject when the sales have different fuel patterns and in-store sales are not a factor in the value estimate.

The comparable sales and the subject are consistent in their expense characteristics below the gross profit line, so the appraiser should be cautious when making these estimates. The sales and the subject should have similar operating expense ratios or similar proportions of income flowing to net income. If the sales and subject are not consistent, this method will produce inaccurate results. Table 7.7 shows the effects on value caused by different operating expense ratios.

Table 7.7 Effects on Value Caused by Different Operating Expense Ratios

	Property A	Property B
Gross profit	$400,000	$400,000
Operating expenses	$300,000	$350,000
Net income to real estate	$100,000	$50,000
Capitalization rate	11%	11%
Value by gross profit multiplier	$1,000,000	$1,000,000
Value by net income capitalization	$909,090	$416,000

In this example, the properties have an identical gross profit of $400,000. However, the operating expense ratios are different: 75% for Property A and 88% for Property B. Using a gross profit multiplier of 2.5 would produce value indications of $1,000,000 for each property. However, if the capitalization were based on the net income to real estate, the resulting value indications would be $909,090 for Property A and $416,000 for Property B. Therefore, stores that appear to be similar at the gross profit level may be quite different at the net income level. A gross profit multiplier can be a useful and important valuation tool, but care must be taken to compare only properties that have operating expense ratios that are similar to the subject's.

Convenience stores vary widely in their physical characteristics, and the appraiser often arrives at a range of values rather than a definitive point estimate. Table 7.8 shows how gross profit multiplier analysis can help the appraiser formulate a conclusion from the indications derived using physical units of comparison.

In Table 7.8 the average indication is $669 per square foot of building area. The median indication is $655, and two indications are $630. The appraiser could reasonably conclude a value using any of these indications. When varying indications are derived, the gross profit multiplier can provide evidence of an appropriate conclusion. For instance, if the calculated value from the gross profit multiplier was $2,700,000, the appraiser might conclude a value of $2,700,000 to $2,720,000, as indicated by Sale 4, even though it is in the upper half of the range.

Table 7.8	Sales Comparison Approach—Arrayed Indications of the Subject's Value per Square Foot of Building Area			
Sale 1	$625	× 4,000 sq. ft.	=	$2,500,000
Sale 2	$630	× 4,000 sq. ft.	=	$2,520,000
Sale 3	$630	× 4,000 sq. ft.	=	$2,520,000
Sale 4	$680	× 4,000 sq. ft.	=	$2,720,000
Sale 5	$710	× 4,000 sq. ft.	=	$2,840,000
Sale 6	$740	× 4,000 sq. ft.	=	$2,960,000

Income Capitalization Approach

According to the National Association of Convenience Stores, fewer than 50% of all convenience stores in the United States are leased and fewer than 30% of all new convenience stores are leased. When stores are leased, the lease arrangement is often a financing tool, not a market-driven agreement. Seldom will the appraiser find an adequate number of truly leased properties on which to base the income capitalization approach. Further, convenience stores are rarely, if ever, sold based on their real estate rental potential. This does not mean, however, that the income capitalization approach cannot be applied to convenience stores. The framework of the income capitalization approach in the appraisal of convenience stores parallels the way industry participants view the real estate. The real estate, like all other assets, is considered in the context of its contribution to earnings.

In classic economic theory, real estate is viewed as one of the four agents of production that creates value: land, labor, capital, and coordination. In the appraisal of a convenience store, the value of the real estate (land) is determined by the convenience store's income potential. This economic view was born out of early classical economics and rent theory. Rent theory holds that land is the last agent in production and its owners receive a return only after all of the other factors of production are satisfied.

The convenience store industry adopts this rent theory in the way it views real estate, except that business profit is considered residual to the land component. The real estate component must be satisfied before profit accrues to the owner. This alteration of rent theory is probably the result of the modern reality that installment mortgages must be paid before the owner-operator enjoys any profit. Today, business practice and laws pertaining to foreclosure require that the real estate mortgage be paid even if nothing else is left for the owner. The profit concept will be discussed later in this section.

The return to real estate is derived from the level of gross sales, the cost of goods sold, and annual operating expenses. To the extent that gross sales are affected by location and the quantity of the improvements and operating expenses are affected by the improvements' management and condition, the store's financial operation becomes a proxy for the real estate's underlying value. Consequently, the real estate analysis begins with the convenience store's annual operating statement. The analysis of operating statements will be explored in more detail later in this chapter. Following is the basic analytical framework of the income capitalization approach as applied to convenience stores.

Gross fuel and in-store sales

Less: Cost of goods sold

Equals: Gross profit

Less: Annual operating expenses

Equals: Net earnings (EBIDTA)*

* In the convenience store industry, net earnings are called *earnings before interest, depreciation, taxes, and amortization (EBIDTA)*.

Capitalizing EBIDTA

Capitalizing EBIDTA provides an indication of the market value of the convenience store operation's going concern. All of the convenience store's tangible and intangible assets are included in the value estimate because they all contribute to EBIDTA.

In addition to including the value of the tangible and intangible assets, capitalization of EBIDTA includes business profit. Together, the tangible assets, intangible assets, and capitalized economic profit (business profit) make up what the Separating Real and Personal Property from Intangible Business Assets course calls the *market value of the total assets of the business (MVTAB)*. MVTAB can be estimated by capitalizing EBIDTA. Capitalization rates can be extracted from the market just as they would be for any other property. However, capitalization of EBIDTA does not distinguish any of the tangible and intangible assets or provide a measure of the contributory value of any of the component parts. For example, capitalization of EBIDTA does not give the appraiser a measure of economic profit or indicate if economic profit even exists. The appraiser must remember that, when capitalizing EBIDTA, any economic profit that exists is included in the value estimate.

The client may ask the appraiser to estimate the real estate's value when a loan will be secured by a real estate mortgage. When the appraiser is required to estimate the value of the real estate associated with a convenience store operation, further refinements to EBIDTA are necessary.[4] EBIDTA components should be separated into their respective economic returns as tangible and intangible assets. These returns (income) are shown in Table 7.9.

A residual income approach can be used to estimate the value of the real property. Once EBIDTA has been determined, the appraiser allocates the portion of the income stream that represents the return to the FF&E and any intangible assets, including capitalized economic profit. The remaining income is the portion of EBIDTA that represents the return to the real estate. This portion of the income stream can then be capitalized by the appraiser into a value estimate for the real estate.

This residual-income economic framework is the basis of the income capitalization approach as applied to convenience stores. It reflects the way the convenience store industry views the role of the real estate in the operation of the business enterprise and the purchase decisions of buyers and sellers of convenience store properties. The remainder of Chapter 7 discusses refining EBIDTA into an income estimate for the real estate.

Table

7.9 | Economic Returns for Tangible and Intangible Assets

Tangible Assets	Classification
Site	Real property
Building	Real property
Fuel service and canopy	Real property or trade fixtures
Furniture, fixtures, and equipment	Trade fixtures or personal property
Inventory	Personal property
Intangible Assets	**Classification**
Franchises and licenses	Non-real property
Skilled workforce	Non-real property
Goodwill	Non-real property
Other	Non-real property

---

4. *Uniform Standards of Professional Appraisal Practice*, Standard Rule 1-4g. As noted earlier, depending on the intended use and user, USPAP requires personal property and intangible items to be separated from real property when developing a real property appraisal.

Calculating EBIDTA

Four steps are followed to calculate earnings before interest, depreciation, taxes, and amortization: estimate gross sales, deduct for shrink, estimate product margins, and deduct annual operating expenses. Calculating EBIDTA is the first step in developing the income capitalization approach for a convenience store.

Estimating Gross Sales

If the property is an existing convenience store, its historical sales levels should be examined. The current year's year-to-date income should be annualized and compared to the last three years' income levels to determine whether the subject store's trend in gross sales is flat, upward, or downward. The appraiser should be sure to remember that road construction, a building expansion, or other unusual circumstances can significantly affect sales in any period. The appraiser should compare the subject's trend to the industry trend using sources such as the State of the Industry Report published by the National Association of Convenience Stores.

As discussed previously, gross sales consist of fuel sales and in-stores sales. Generally the direction of fuel sales and in-store sales are the same. It is unusual for in-store sales to move upward while fuel sales are moving downward. It is generally not necessary to break out the different grades of gasoline. In-store sales include all sales other than fuel sales: merchandise, food service, and other, such as carwash income. Income categories have different margins and must be tracked separately. If the price of a particular product category, such as cigarettes or gasoline, jumps significantly in one year, the gross sales will appear much higher than the previous year's gross sales. However, the increase in gross sales will not usually affect gross profit. These volatile movements occur at the wholesale level and are in turn reflected in retail prices. If anything looks unusual in the subject's pattern of gross sales over the last few years, the appraiser should ask the owner-operator about it.

Deducting for Shrink

Shrink is product loss caused by damage or the expiration of the product's freshness date. A percentage allowance for shrink is deducted from gross sales. A 1% allowance is typical, but sometimes the percentage is higher than 1%. Shrink of more than 2% is unusual.

Estimating Product Margins

The *product margin* is how much income remains after paying the wholesale cost of the merchandise. The annual wholesale cost to the store is commonly called the *cost of goods sold* on the operating statement. Fuel margins for each grade of gasoline may be different, but they are aggregated into one average called the *pool margin*. Typically, pool margins are about 9% to 13%; they may be less in a highly competitive market with hypermarkets. In-store margins are usually higher than fuel margins and typically range from 28% to 34%.

The appraiser should ask the owner-operator about the subject's historical margins and compare the historical margins to industry standards. Margins can and do change from year to year, but historically category margins have stayed within a comparatively narrow range.

If the subject's historical margins are extraordinarily low, the retail prices at the subject store may be too low. In a highly competitive market, margins would be expected to be lower. For example, the industry reports that fuel margins at competing convenience stores commonly drop to 0% to 4% when a hypermarket such as Wal-Mart begins selling gasoline.

The national average product margins for nearly everything sold in a convenience store can be found in sources such as the State of the Industry Report published by the National Association of Convenience Stores. For proposed stores, the margins must be projected. Projected margins for new stores must be consistent with information reported in the earlier sections of the appraisal report that analyze market supply and demand. If the subject's market is oversupplied and has a location quotient of 0.75, projecting margins higher than the industry average would be inappropriate.

The margin's mathematical complement is the cost of goods sold. If the pool margin for fuel is 10%, the cost of goods sold for the fuel category is 90%. The appraiser should use the margin to compute the dollar amount of the cost of goods sold for each category. The appraiser then deducts shrink and the cost of goods sold from gross sales to arrive at gross profit.

Using the fuel margins identified above, assume that a store has $1,000,000 in fuel sales for the year. The computation of net sales is

> Fuel sales $1,000,000
>
> Less: Cost of goods sold $900,000
>
> Less: Shrink (1%) $10,000
>
> Gross profit $90,000

Notice that shrink is deducted from total sales rather than from gross profit. The cost of goods sold is figured from gross sales, not gross sales after the shrink allowance has been deducted. Completing the arithmetic in this order is important because the owner-operator absorbs all of the shrink loss and pays all of the wholesale costs.

Deducting Annual Operating Expenses

After deducting shrink and the cost of goods sold, the owner-operator pays the annual operating expenses, which include the items listed below. In figuring the percentage allowance for each of the following items, the industry makes the percentage calculation from total sales before shrink. The appraiser should compare the subject's operating performance to published convenience store industry averages. For example, the State of the Industry Report is published every year. The operating expense categories below reflect the way the industry categorizes stores' operating expenses. With the help of industry standards, the appraiser's task of establishing and common sizing operating expenses for the reconstructed statement is comparatively easy. *Common sizing* is the practice of analyzing the owner's operating statement by calculating the annual itemized expense as a percent of gross sales. It is a better way to track trends in operating expenses than simply looking at nominal dollar amounts.

With the exception of labor costs, the numbers in the labor expense category are relatively small. The total of all items in the labor expense category should be approximately 7% to 13% of total sales. Because labor costs are the largest component of operating expenses, the appraiser should carefully consider and verify them as much as possible. It may not be appropriate to use the actual historical wages on the owner's operating statement because they may not accurately reflect any wages the owner has taken out of the business.

Labor Costs. *Labor* is usually the largest category of annual operating expenses on the owner's operating statement. Labor expense includes all employee compensation. Wages, payroll taxes, workers' compensation, health insurance, and other employee benefits are grouped together.

The owner's profits are not expensed with labor costs but are considered later as part of the profit allowance. The appraiser will have to use good judgment if the store is a "mom and pop" operation and the owners are the only employees. In this instance, a fair wage should be deducted for what would normally be paid to employees. If the owner contributes personal labor to the store's operation, the allowance deducted from the labor costs should reflect the opportunity cost of that level of labor contribution, whether it is an entry level wage or the potentially high cost of hiring a store manager.

Later in the analysis of EBIDTA, an allowance is made for owner profit. Owner profit is separate and distinct from the owner's wages. The labor expense category can vary widely from one store to another depending on how labor-intensive the operation is. A full-size, co-branded restaurant requires more employees than a self-serve food operation does. Labor costs usually range from 4% to 9%.

Insurance. *Insurance* includes liability and business insurance, but not fire coverage for the real estate improvements. The insurance allowance is usually 0.1% to 0.5% of total sales.

Royalty Fees. The appraiser should not confuse royalty fees with franchise fees. A *franchise fee* is an upfront charge the operator pays to use the licensed concept. For example, Burger King usually charges $37,500 for a franchise. *Royalties* and *advertising fees* are ongoing payments to the franchisor to cover administrative and marketing costs. They are annual fees based on a percentage of gross or net sales. The appraiser must remember that a QSR royalty will be based on food service sales, not on fuel sales. QSR royalty fees range from 4% to 8% of food service sales. Royalties for an operation are usually 0.1% to 0.2% of gross sales.

Advertising Fees. Some operations spend little on advertising; others have billboards, radio spots, and newspaper advertisements. Advertising expenses often reflect the operator's business philosophy. Advertising is one of the few items the operator may consider an optional expense. It can vary widely and be cut drastically in a year of poor revenue. Typically, an allowance of 0.1% to 0.2% of total sales is appropriate for operations that do not have nationally branded food service.

The advertising costs of nationally branded food service, such as McDonald's or Wendy's, are specified in the franchise agreement and figured as a percentage of either gross or net food service sales. Some companies combine royalties and advertising into a single payment. Industry averages for advertising apart from the amounts included in royalty fees are about 0.3% of gross sales.

Supplies. *Supplies* include all purchases of items not for resale that are used in the management and operation of the business. Cleaning products and office supplies fall into the supply category. This category usually ranges from 0.5% to 0.7% of gross sales.

Utilities. *Utilities* include water, sewage, electricity, and natural gas. Appraisers should know that some heating requirements can be met using the heat emitted by refrigeration compressors. The heat emitted by refrigeration compressors is often recycled to heat a building in cold weather. BP Oil Company is experimenting with mounting PV solar panels on their canopies to generate electricity. The company asserts that 10% to 20% of a convenience store's electrical needs can be supplied by PV solar panels. Usually utilities constitute 1.0% of total sales.

Motor Fuel Drive-Offs. The convenience store industry tracks motor fuel drive-offs in a separate expense category. Motor fuel drive-offs increase when fuel prices are high. According to industry averages, motor fuel drive-offs accounted for 0.1% of gross sales in 2000.

Cash Short/Over. As with most retail sales businesses, cash balances for the year are usually reconciled in a separate account on the annual statement. *Cash short* means that less money came into the cash register than should have. The appraiser will usually find the operating statement lists a "cash short" amount, rather than a "cash over" amount. Cash short typically comprises 0.1% of gross sales, according to industry averages.

Other. Non-categorized, miscellaneous items can be figured at 1.2% of total sales. In addition to the items discussed above, the convenience store appraiser will frequently find deductions for depreciated book value, store rent, repairs, maintenance, and mortgage interest on the actual operating statement because these items are eligible for income tax deductions. Depreciated book value and mortgage interest should not be included as expense items. Although depreciated book value and mortgage interest are legitimate income tax deductions, they are not included on the appraiser's reconstructed statement as developed here. The appraiser cannot compare the overall percentage of operating expenses on the reconstructed statement to the published industry average because the published industry average will include items that the appraiser has not included in the reconstructed operating statement.

After deducting annual operating expenses for net sales, the convenience store appraiser arrives at net earnings, or the earnings before interest, depreciation, taxes, and amortization (EBIDTA). Capitalizing EBIDTA provides an indication of the market value of the total assets of the business (MVTAB) as if sold in aggregate or as a going concern.

The capitalization rate for developing MVTAB can be extracted from sales of convenience stores when EBIDTA is developed for the sale property. EBIDTA is divided by the sale price. Typically, the R_{TAB} (capitalization rate for the market value of the total assets of the business) will be higher than R_O, the overall capitalization rate of the real estate only. The theoretical reasons for the difference in capitalization rates include the shorter economic lives of FF&E and the higher investment risk associated with intangible assets such as capitalized economic profit (CEP).

Separating Real Estate Value from EBIDTA

Most business appraisers allocate the income to the real estate by presuming that the real estate's value is already known. Business appraisers commonly rely on real estate appraisers to estimate the value of the real estate. Once the value of the real estate is known, the business appraiser then allocates that portion of the business income that represents a return to the real estate. After also deducting the economic return to any other tangible assets, such as trade equipment, the amount of income remaining represents the economic return to the intangible assets of the business. But what if the value of the real estate is not known? Can the appraiser estimate the value of the real estate for a convenience store by examining the income stream to the overall business enterprise?

The answer is, yes. The appraiser quantifies the income that can reasonably be allocated to the other tangible assets and to the intangible assets. The income remaining after the allocation is that portion of EBIDTA that is generated by the real estate. Following the discussion in the Appraisal Institute's Separating Real and

Personal Property from Intangible Assets course, the identification of tangible and intangible assets and the profit component for a convenience store operation may be thought of as follows:

1. Real property
   Land, site improvements (parking, forecourt paving, canopy) and building or buildings (store, fuel dispensers, USTs, QSR, carwash structure)

2. Tangible personal property or FF&E
   Freestanding coolers and freezers, shelving, gondolas, food service cookers, freestanding stainless steel sinks, hot dog rollers, tables, chairs, computers, office equipment, inventory, etc.

3. Intangible business assets
   Cash and equivalents, assembled workforce, business name, non-realty contracts, innovations.

Economic profit is all revenue not captured as a return on the value of the real property, tangible personal property, or any other intangible asset of the going concern. The authors of the Separating Real and Personal Property from Intangible Assets course state:

> ...economic profit is a residual claimed by entrepreneurial activity (risk taking and/or innovation). It is what remains after satisfying the opportunity cost claims of all agents of production embodied in the going concern.[5]

Residual Real Estate Income Allocation

The income allocation with real estate as the residual can be performed by making the following deductions to EBIDTA:

> EBIDTA
> – Tangible assets, non-realty such as FF&E income
> = Residual income to real property, intangible assets, and economic profit

The intangible assets and economic profit are deducted from the remaining income to isolate the portion of the subject's income that provides an economic return to the real estate.

Deducting Return for Other Tangible Assets and FF&E

Part of the revenue that a convenience store generates originates from the personal property, non-realty equipment, and other tangible, non-real estate items used in the operation of the business. A deduction is made for the portion of the income stream attributable to non-realty items. When a full-size fast-food restaurant such

---

5.   See the Appraisal Institute's Course 800, Separating Real and Personal Property from Intangible Assets, 5-8.

as a 2-in-1 is present, the equipment value can be as much as 16% of the real estate's value. For smaller QSRs and stores with no branded food service, the value of equipment is considerably less. The deduction for income to furnishings, fixtures, and equipment represents the economic return required by the quantity and quality of FF&E that is present in the operation.

The economic return can be calculated in one of two ways. The value of the equipment can be estimated and an annual economic return allowance can be calculated, or an allowance for the annual return to equipment can be made based on a percentage of net earnings. An appropriate annual return for FF&E would be 15% to 20%, based on a 10% return on invested capital in FF&E and considering a life expectancy of 10 to 15 years. The net earnings allocation to FF&E would be between 1% and 5%. The process for calculating the economic return to the equipment is shown in Table 7.10

Either of these methods can produce the same allocation to FF&E. As discussed in Chapter 6, estimating the value of used equipment can be difficult for the real estate appraiser. The return on value method can more readily be applied to new equipment.

If the equipment's value cannot be determined, an allocation of net earnings may be used by the appraiser. Once the income allocation to the equipment has been made, the appraiser can check the results. The appraiser should simply capitalize the income to equipment at an appropriate rate to produce an estimate of value for the FF&E.

Although the convenience store appraiser estimates the equipment's value as part of the process of deriving the income to real estate, the appraiser must be cautious when applying these results to a professional opinion of equipment value. The real estate appraiser should not offer a conclusion about the equipment's value that the client regards as a professional opinion.

Table

7.10   Calculating the Economic Return to Equipment

Income to FF&E Based of/on Return of Value

$30,000 value of FF&E

18% economic rate of/on return

$5,400 annual economic return

The deduction from EBIDTA for FF&E is $5,400.

Income to FF&E Based on Allocation of EBIDTA

$225,546 net earnings

2.5% allocation

$5,638 annual economic return

The deduction from EBIDTA for FF&E is $5,600.

Deducting Intangible Asset Returns and Business Profit

The deduction for intangible asset returns and business profit is one of the most challenging and subjective judgments in convenience store appraisal. No simple formula or multiplier can be applied that is appropriate for every store. Moreover, the profit margins of the past may not reflect the current market. The appraiser should be aware that, in this residual allocation to real estate, what is not classified as intangible asset returns and business profit will flow to the real property and FF&E. In other words, the less income allowed for profit, the more income flows to the tangible assets. Consequently, when the income stream to the real estate is capitalized, it will indicate a lower or higher value to the real estate, depending on how much income was allocated to intangible asset returns and business profit.

All of the previous computations used to arrive at net earnings were fairly straight-forward. They were achieved with simple arithmetic and can be easily corroborated. At this point the appraiser's task becomes more difficult. In estimating the economic return to the intangible assets and business profit, the appraiser must use skill, judgment, experience, and common sense. If up to this point the methodology of convenience store appraising could have been called science, at this point it becomes art.

The appraiser must ask, "Do the tangible assets receive the business's economic return first?" In other words, do the tangible assets have a priority economic claim over the intangible assets? This is largely an irrelevant question when the business operates at a profit. However, when the business does not earn a profit, this question can be vitally important. Business appraisers state that the tangible assets receive their economic return first, before any other assets of the business. A commonly used business appraisal method is the excess earnings method. In *Guide to Business Valuations,*[6] the authors state that intangible assets earn a return only after the economic return requirements for the tangible assets have been satisfied. In other words, the business's intangible assets have value only if there are excess earnings.

In allocating income, the investment requirements of the tangible assets are satisfied first, then the intangible assets. Finally, business profit remains. If the business does not have excess earnings but provides enough economic return to meet the requirements of the tangible assets, the intangible assets have no value and no business profit exists. Intangible assets and profit always have a secondary, or subordinate, claim on earnings to the tangible assets.

Some convenience store operations will have no profit. In the highly competitive and saturated markets that most stores operate in today, few stores will have excess earnings.

The profit allowed on the reconstructed statement should also be consistent with the appraiser's previous allocation of any labor contributed by the owner-operator. Frequently, the owner-operator contributes labor to the business's operation. If the appraiser made no wage allowance for the owner under labor costs, the

---

6. Jay E. Fishman, Shannon Pratt, et al., *Guide to Business Valuations,* 12th ed. (Fort Worth: Practitioners Publishing Company, 2000), 7-28.

allowance for owner's compensation must be made at this time. In many markets today, after allowing for working wages for the owner or owners, little or no business profit remains. In other words, the operation of the convenience store only allows the owner or owners to make wages and pay bills.

Indications that intangible value and business profits exist in a convenience store operation may include

- Gross profits significantly above industry norms
- Location quotients higher than one
- Capitalized EBIDTA values that are higher than the replacement cost less depreciation of the tangible assets plus land value

Indications that no returns are available for intangible assets or business profit could include

- A pattern of declining gross profits over the past several years
- Location quotients substantially lower than one
- New competition since the time of the subject's original construction
- The opening of a Wal-Mart fuel center or other mass merchandiser selling motor fuel within the subject's market

These are only indications. The comments of the owner and other competitors in the area will also help the appraiser determine whether the local trade area is profitable for convenience store operators. During interviews with buyers and sellers, the appraiser will ask how much of the sale price is attributable to intangible business value. The answer to this question affects the allocation of the subject's income to intangible assets and business profit.

Estimating the subject store's profit is difficult, so it is important for the convenience store appraiser to closely follow the convenience store industry and the issues that convenience store operators confront. If the appraiser understands and recognizes these factors, he or she can exercise the skill and judgment required in allocating earnings to intangible assets and profit. For example, during the boom years of the 1980s and 1990s, the convenience store industry was experiencing rapid growth in sales and gross profits. As expected, new stores were constructed on almost every good corner. Nearly every store made a profit. The situation today is dramatically different. With market saturation of existing stores and mass merchandisers gaining market share in fuel sales, store profits are minimal and even nonexistent for many operations. The industry is struggling and it is rare to encounter a store with significant excess earnings.

The appraiser cannot make a mechanical allocation for profit simply because the estimate derived represents the business's total assets. For example, in one actual assignment a convenience store appraiser determined that a proposed convenience store and truck fueling facility in a small rural town was not financially feasible. The determination was based on the appraiser's calculation that the capitalized EBIDTA would be insufficient to cover the cost of the real property assets. The appraiser demonstrated this fact with a projection that the capitalized EBIDTA would approximate $500,000 and the cost new of the improvements plus land value was more than $1,200,000. Clearly, the proposed project was not feasible. However, the appraiser went on to allocate a substantial amount of projected income to "business profit." This was a mistake. No business profit can exist in a situation where the investment requirements of the tangible assets are not met. If the project is not feasible in the first place, how can it be making a profit? The appraiser was simply not thinking about these issues and made an artificial, unsupported allowance for profit when none was warranted.

Under the most favorable industry operating conditions, returns to intangible assets and business profit will constitute no more than 15% to 20% of gross profit, which is about 30% to 35% of EBIDTA. Some economic return is required for the real and personal property and it too must be allocated.

The convenience store appraiser can employ a sensitivity analysis to gauge the resulting effect of various profit allocations on the real estate's value. Table 7.11 shows three examples of an income allocation to intangible assets and business profit. The examples show how different allocations can affect the residual income to the real estate.

Note that the residual income to real estate gets smaller as the profit allowance increases. Consequently, the capitalized value of the residual income declines as more of the earnings are allocated to intangibles and business profit. The appraiser must recognize the inverse relationship between the allowance to intangible assets and business profit and real estate value.

The convenience store industry records annual profit margins in publications such as the State of the Industry Report. The published pre-tax profit can be used as

Table

7.11 Allocation of Return on Intangible Assets and Business Profit

	No Profit Allowance 0%*	Moderate Profit Allowance 10%*	High Profit Allowance 20%*
EBIDTA	$200,000	$200,000	$200,000
Return on intangible assets and business profit	$0	$20,000	$40,000
Residual return to real estate	$200,000	$180,000	$160,000
Real estate cap rate	12.0%	12.0%	12.0%
Real estate value	$1,666,666	$1,500,000	$1,333,333

*As a percent of EBIDTA

an industry proxy for the allowance for intangibles and business profit. Although the pre-tax profit is computed differently by the industry, it can be a useful yardstick for illustrating industry trends. The appraiser is advised not to use the pre-tax profit in direct comparison to the return allowance for intangible assets and business profit. In 2000 the pre-tax profit was 14.3% of gross profit adjusted for interest expense.

When the appraiser's analysis of the convenience store industry and the subject's trade area indicate that no excess profits exist, the appraiser can begin the income allocation analysis assuming no allowance for a return to intangible assets and no profit for the subject store. The resulting value estimate for the real estate can then be compared to the indications from the cost and sales comparison approaches. If the preliminary value indication for the store's real estate appears too high, incremental increases in the profit allowance can be made to reduce the economic return to the real estate. For example, if the first allocation resulted in a value to the real estate that was higher than the site's value and the replacement cost of the improvements, the allocation of income to the real estate is too high.

Capitalizing Remaining Income to Real Estate

After deducting allowances for a return to FF&E, intangible assets, and business profit, the remaining income accrues to the real estate. The industry considers the real estate to be the land, buildings, and fuel service. From the real estate income the appraiser makes further deductions for maintenance and repairs and for the reserve requirement of the real estate improvements. The deductions for real estate expenses are treated just as they are in appraisals of other types of real estate. At this point, the appraiser capitalizes the remaining income into a value estimate for the real estate.

The capitalization rate is best derived from the sales used in the sales comparison approach. As discussed earlier in this chapter, the appraiser should collect sales operating income data in addition to the sale price and physical description of the property. Now the operating information from the comparable sale properties can be used in developing overall capitalization rate estimates for the subject property. To develop market-based capitalization rates, an operating income analysis should be performed for every sale that was used in the sales comparison approach. The use of electronic spreadsheets simplifies the calculations. Real estate capitalization rates for convenience stores are usually between 9% and 14%.

The appraiser should be cautious when applying someone else's capitalization rate to the income stream developed. To be consistent, capitalization rates must be developed and extracted from the comparables in the same way they were derived for the subject. A trade association's definition of net income may be different than the appraiser's. A proprietary database may calculate net income differently than the appraisal industry. Inaccurate value estimates may result from developing the income to real estate and then applying a capitalization rate that was supplied by a third party. Unless the appraiser knows exactly how the third party calculated the net income, third-party sources are not useful in supplying capitalization rates. For example, although the National Association of Convenience Stores does not provide capitalization rates, it does provide nationwide averages for pre-tax profit. The appraiser might be tempted to try to use the pre-tax profit in the profit allocation of net earnings. However, it is difficult to ascertain how the pre-tax profit was calculated. Similarly, the convenience store industry's definition of lease income cannot be directly applied to the appraisal of convenience stores.

An operating income analysis and capitalization are illustrated in Table 7.12 and Table 7.13. Three columns are shown so the appraiser can visually compare the industry standard and actual subject performance to the appraiser's projection of sales and operating expenses.

Because the operating expense section of this example closely parallels the industry standard expense categories as published by the National Association of Convenience Stores, it facilitates direct comparison of the subject's operating performance to published industry benchmarks. However, for appraisal purposes some modifications to the NACS operating expense model are necessary.

In creating the reconstructed operating statement, the appraiser should exclude the following expenses published by the NACS:

- Personal property taxes
- Depreciation/amortization
- Store rent
- Equipment rent
- Repair and maintenance

These expense items are excluded because the appraiser will make subsequent computations to the income stream that pertain to personal and real property. As a result, the appraiser must not deduct the above expense items at this point in the analysis. In the NACS expense benchmark, the items in the above list generally total 4% to 6% of gross sales. The appraiser should recognize that the typical NACS operating expense total published in the State of the Industry Report will be 400 to 600 basis points higher than the appraiser's reconstructed total annual operating expenses as a percent of gross sales.

When Convenience Stores Fail to Perform

Convenience stores are income-producing properties. All of the physical elements that constitute the property's assets are assembled to generate income. For certain properties, the business's earnings may be insufficient to provide an economic re-

Table

7.12 Reconstructed Operating Statement

		Projection		Actual Amount Stabilized	Industry Standard*
Estimated gallons per year		1,180,000		1,180,287	1,014,000
Average price/gallon		$1.50		$1.50	$1.50
Fuel dollars		$1,770,000		$1,770,431	$1,199,00
Merchandise (in-store) sales		$737,000		$737,000	$757,000
Food service		$0		$0	
Carwash		$0		$0	
Other		$0		$0	
Total sales		$2,507,000		$2,507,431	
Shrink	1.00%	$25,070	1.00%	$25,074	
Cost of goods sold:					
Fuel	88%	$1,542,024	88%	$1,542,399	89%
Merchandise	68%	$496,148	68%	$496,148	68%
Food service	35%	$0	35%	$0	
Carwash	20%	$0	20%	$0	
Other	0%	$0	0%	$0	
Margin	18%		18%		20%
Gross profit		$443,758		$443,809	
Less operating expenses:					
Labor costs	7.00%	$175,490	7.00%	$175,500	7.0%
Liability insurance	0.10%	$2,507	0.10%	$2,500	0.1%
Royalty fees	0.10%	$2,507	0.10%	$2,500	0.1%
Supplies	0.59%	$14,791	0.59%	$14,794	0.5%
Advertising	0.30%	$7,521	0.30%	$7,500	0.3%
Utilities	1.00%	$25,070	1.00%	$25,000	1.0%
Motor fuel drive-offs	0.10%	$2,507	0.10%	$2,500	0.1%
Cash short/over	0.10%	$2,507	0.10%	$2,500	0.1%
Other	1.20%	$30,084	1.20%	$30,000	1.2%
Subtotal	10.49%	$262,894	10.48%	$262,794	10.4%
EBIDTA**	7.21%	$180,773	7.22%	$181,015	

* Industry standard in NACS State of the Industry Report for 2000.

** EBIDTA is earnings before interest, depreciation, taxes, and amortization.

Table

7.13 Projected Operating Profile Summary

Gross sales	100%	$2,507,000
Cost of goods sold	81%	$2,038,172
Operating expenses/shrink	11%	$288,054
EBIDTA	7%	$180,773

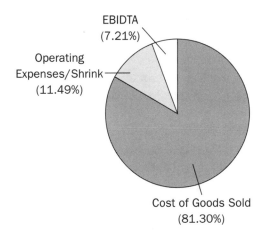

EBIDTA
(7.21%)

Operating
Expenses/Shrink
(11.49%)

Cost of Goods Sold
(81.30%)

Contribution to Gross Profit

Gross profit	$443,758
Add: shrink	$25,070
	$468,828

Contribution Categories		**Contribution Ratios**
Fuel	$227,976	49%
Merchandise	$240,852	51%
Food service	$0	0%
Carwash	$0	0%
Other	$0	0%
		100%

turn to all or part of the tangible assets. With increasing frequency, convenience stores today are not earning enough income to justify their investment in land, buildings, and fuel service. The factors that contribute to convenience stores' lack of income are market saturation, an insufficient population base, and new competitive channels.

Market Saturation

Market saturation is the overbuilding of convenience stores in a particular market. It may be characterized by location quotients below 50%. With the excessive building of the 1990s, market saturation is now becoming evident. Over the short term, convenience stores in an oversupplied market will typically have below-average fuel and in-store margins as operators cut retail prices to compete. Over the long term, failing stores will close and supply and demand will become balanced.

The appraiser should not assume that only old stores in a particular market close. The stores that are best able to operate with reduced earnings will survive. A new store with a cost of $2,000,000 that is highly leveraged and unable to meet its debt payments may be forced to close before an old store that is debt-free. In an oversupplied market, the appraiser cannot always predict which stores will close and which will remain open.

Insufficient Population Base

Sometimes stores have been built in towns that are too small to support them. In one example, an operator built a $250,000 store in a town of 400 people. The store failed to perform and the income could not cover the mortgage payments. The community was simply too small to provide enough revenue to justify the investment. A smaller store costing $100,000 could have performed well. In this case the store was simply overbuilt for the market.

New Competitive Channels

The single biggest problem in the industry today is fuel sales competition from mass merchandisers and grocery chains such as Wal-Mart, CostCo, and Alberston's. Until 2000, most of these retailers did not sell gasoline. Today, nearly every retail chain is entering the fuel sales business. Even Jack-in-the-Box fast-food restaurants are experimenting with a restaurant/fuel sales concept. Often these new entrants are using discounted and even predatory gasoline pricing to gain market share. The success of these new fuel retailers is undermining the convenience store industry.

Many local, modestly capitalized convenience store operators are being driven out of the fuel sales business. The convenience store industry is frantically searching for new profit centers, such as dry cleaning service, banking, and food offerings, to replace the lost fuel dollars that will likely never return. In markets where fuel margins were once 13 cents or more per gallon, it is common to see margins today below four cents, sometimes even down to zero.

When appraisers encounter a problem store, the first question they should ask is, "What is the source of the problem?" They should start by talking to the owner because owners can be surprisingly candid about the troubles they are having. The appraiser must determine if the store's poor performance is the result of poor management or if it is market-related. If the problem is market-related, the property value is being impacted and the appraiser will have to indicate this in the analysis.

The appraiser should be able to spot trends that show declines in gross sales and margins. Single-year fluctuations are normal. A consistent downward trend over a period of three to five years indicates that economic problems exist.

The subject's sales and profitability performance should be compared to industry standards and trends as described in Chapter 1. In the United States, store averages for several performance measures are published annually by trade organizations such as the National Association of Convenience Stores. Examples of operating industry benchmarks are shown in Table 7.14.

Data on industry averages is crucial to convenience store appraisal. Knowing industry averages helps the appraiser establish benchmarks for the subject store's performance. Trade organizations often track operating data over several years. Consequently, the appraiser can easily compare the subject's three- to five-year history to industry trends. Profitability benchmarks that are published annually by NACS are shown in Table 7.15.

Table 7.14 **Examples of Industry Benchmarks**

2000 Industry Averages	
In-store sales per store	$870,000
Motor fuel sales per store	$1,807,000
Motor fuel gallons per store	1,262,000
Operating income per store	$99,100
Pre-tax profit per store	$38,300
Margins	
In-store gross profit margin	28.4%
Motor fuel gross profit margin	9.3%
Combined gross profit margin	16.8%
Motor fuel gross profit (cents per gallon)	$0.133

Table 7.15 **2000 Profitability Statistics**

As a Percent of Total Sales	
Gross profit	14.8%
Pre-tax profit	1.7%
Operating income	$99,100
EBIDTA	$90,100
Pre-tax profit	$38,300

After the appraiser determines the operating trends for the subject, the next step is to compare the nominal dollar figures to the industry averages. If the subject's nominal performance is falling substantially below national averages, it is likely the subject is a problem property.

What if the store's economic return is less than a reasonable rate of return on the tangible assets, which include the site, building, fuel service, FF&E, and inventory? This situation is called *negative goodwill*. Negative goodwill indicates that the market value of the subject store's going concern is less than the sum of the individual values of the store's total tangible assets. When negative goodwill exists, the subject store's income is insufficient to justify buying the store on the basis of the collective value of its individual tangible assets. The negative market value of the goodwill at least partially offsets the positive value of the tangible assets.

Should the net asset value fall below the liquidation value of the store's assets, the appraiser will conclude that the business, and thus the store, is worth more on a liquidation basis than on a going-concern basis. In other words, a liquidation of the subject business would be a rational economic choice and the highest and best use of the property. The two types of liquidation are orderly disposition liquidation and forced liquidation. In an *orderly disposition liquidation,* the store's assets are sold off separately, not as an assemblage or whole property. It is assumed that adequate exposure and marketing time is allowed to market the assets. A *forced liquidation* is similar to an orderly disposition liquidation in that the assets are sold off in a piecemeal fashion. However, a forced liquidation assumes an abnormally short marketing time. It also assumes that the assets are sold at auction. The bidders at the auction may not represent all potential buyers in the market. The forced liquidation assumes no contributory value from the tangible assets to the intangible assets and vice-versa.

For failing convenience stores, an orderly disposition liquidation or forced liquidation will result in the physical and legal separation of the real estate from the FF&E and inventory. To dispose of the real estate, the fuel service may also be segregated and removed from the site and building component. Typically, the underground storage tanks will be decommissioned or removed. Fuel dispensers and, occasionally, canopies will be removed so the building and site can be marketed for another use. Since convenience stores are usually located in high-traffic areas, alternative uses sometimes include retail stores, fast-food restaurants, and offices. Figure 7.7 shows what was left after a Shell-branded store ceased business operations. All that remains of the tangible assets are the site, building shell, and canopy. It is not unusual for the appraiser to discover that welded steel canopies have little or no resale value. The cost of disassembly and transportation usually outweighs any salvage or transferable market value the canopy would have.

In Figure 7.7, the fuel dispensers have been removed and the building and site are available for alternative uses. The appraiser must remember that the contribu-

7.7 A View of a Closed Convenience Store

tory value of a remaining canopy is probably low when the alternative uses are retail stores, restaurants, or offices. In Figure 7.7 the canopy actually interferes with on-site parking and traffic flow. The canopy may be a burden that the new property owner will pay to have removed. Similarly, the fuel dispensers and underground storage tanks usually have no transferable market value. The appraiser should check with knowledgeable fuel equipment suppliers in the local area. Even modern equipment can have a minimum transferable market value. One of the reasons for the minimal value is the high cost of disassembling the equipment and transporting it to another location.

Decommissioning USTs involves a formal administrative procedure. The government agency overseeing the underground storage tank program maintains records on each operating UST within the state. Every UST is considered active and the owner, operator, or both are legally responsible for the UST until the UST is formally decommissioned or closed. Decommissioning procedures involve several administrative requirements. Physical aspects of decommissioning include closing the UST onsite by draining the tank and filling it with an inert material such as concrete slurry, foam, or sand. The Environmental Protection Agency recommends removing the UST from the site because a soil sample directly under the tank must be tested for contamination. The appraiser should contact the appropriate state agency, which is usually the Department of Environmental Quality, to check the status of contamination issues and any UST problems remaining on a closed or non-operating convenience store property. Typically, new fuel dispensers at failed stores will have a transferable market value of only 10 to 20 cents on the dollar value of the equipment when it was new. Older technology has no value.

Once a troubled convenience store's tangible assets have been separated into marketable units, the site and building shell can be marketed like any other property. Under the terms of the liquidation, the site and building may be auctioned with minimal marketing time or the remaining real estate may be listed and sold through conventional means. The appraiser should understand and clearly identify the marketing assumptions for failed stores.

Conclusion

The convenience industry is experiencing its most turbulent period since the oil embargo of the 1970s. Changes such as rapidly declining fuel sales are taking place that will forever transform this industry. For more than 20 years, fuel sales have accounted for roughly 50% of convenience store revenues. Now that is changing, and it is difficult to predict how long it will be before the industry looks entirely different than it does today. The appraiser needs to be aware that old rules simply cannot be applied to appraising stores today.

The convenience industry is a complex and fascinating retail channel. The challenge for convenience store appraisers is to keep abreast of the changes taking place and to understand how real estate value is created in this industry.

Sources of Data

Statistical data on store development, fuel and merchandise sales, and operating margins

State of the Industry Report, published annually

National Association of Convenience Stores

1600 Duke Street

Alexandria, VA 22314

(703) 684-3600

Industry Report

Convenience Store News

770 Broadway Ave.

New York, NY 10003

Subscriptions: (847) 647-7987

Glossary

2-in-1. A building design that features a full-size fast-food restaurant and a full-size convenience store. These buildings typically have 4,000 square feet of space or more.

additional profit centers (APCs). Concepts such as video rental stores, pharmacies, and fax/copy services that are incorporated into a store's design to supplement the store's fuel and merchandise revenues.

aluminum composite material (ACM) panel. A type of pre-engineered exterior building material consisting of three layers. The material is lighter than many other building materials and can be used to form curves on a building's exterior.

annual sales per square foot. The average unit volume divided by the square footage of the operation. The annual sales per square foot typically is used in the industry to compare restaurant units within the same menu segment.

automatic traffic recording station (ATR station). A place near the subject store where comprehensive information about traffic volume and traffic patterns is recorded.

average daily traffic (ADT). A term found in traffic count data that describes the amount of traffic passing through a specific area.

average unit volume (AUV). A tool restaurants use to gauge performance and potential profitability. The average unit volume depends on the size of the QSR, the size of the average check, and whether the unit is located off a highway or in a residential area.

blender dispenser. A type of fuel dispenser that allows fuels of different octane grades to be blended at a manifold in the dispenser.

breakeven analysis. A useful analytical tool that shows the minimum sales a convenience store operator will need to pay for the added expense of a carwash.

breakplace store. A store in which the store's operator receives management and design assistance from an oil company.

canopy. A structure that gives a convenience store an identity. Canopies provide shelter and can effectively advertise a brand through their color and design.

capture rate. The number of cars that use a carwash. It is expressed as a percentage of the average daily traffic count that passes by the store.

cash short. A situation in which less money comes into the cash register than should.

co-branding. An arrangement in which a restaurant and convenience store locate on the same parcel, resulting in lower land costs and development costs. Co-branding allows a convenience store to locate on a site that otherwise would be too costly.

convenience store specialists. Food service programs designed specifically for convenience stores.

cost of goods sold. The annual wholesale cost of goods to a convenience store.

drive-time study. A map that shows driving times to the subject store. Areas of equal drive-time are colored the same. A drive-time study may show the geographic areas within a one-minute, three-minute, and five-minute drive of the subject, considering existing transportation routes, speed limits, and traffic control devices around the subject property.

dual-product dispenser. A dispenser that has two separate mechanical structures for dispensing fuel in one shell.

economic profit. All revenue not captured as a return on the value of the real property, tangible personal property, or any intangible asset of the going concern.

electronic dispenser. A fuel dispenser that has a digital display showing the total sale and gallons of fuel dispensed during a transaction. Electronic dispensers can be reprogrammed quickly to adapt to changes in fuel prices.

end cap. A separate merchandise display unit located on the end of a shelf. Usually the merchandise is displayed at a right angle to the aisle.

expanded convenience store. Stores that have 2,800 to 3,600 square feet of space. They can accommodate shelving for additional grocery products or room for a fast-food operation and seating.

exterior insulation finish system (EIFS). An external insulation system consisting of rigid foam insulation with waterproof stucco siding applied over the top.

exterior-only carwash. A type of automated carwash with a long, tunnel-like bay. The vehicle is driven into the entrance and the front tire, usually on the driver's side, is positioned on a special conveyor belt that pulls the vehicle through the tunnel.

exterior-rollover carwash. A type of automated carwash in which the vehicle is driven into the center of the building and robotic equipment washes the vehicle. Exterior-rollover carwashes can be located on sites too small to accommodate exterior-only systems.

far corner. A corner that is located on the other side of a traffic control device as one approaches the intersection.

food service. Fresh food prepared onsite.

food service equipment. The personal property associated with the preparation, display, and sale of proprietary or nonbranded food service items in a convenience store. Food service equipment includes cookers, warmers, sinks, and heated display units, but not equipment used for merchandise display such as walk-in beverage coolers.

forecourt. The portion of the convenience store site between the street frontage and the front of the store. Customer parking and fuel service are usually located in the forecourt.

four-square design. A common fuel service layout in which fueling positions are arranged in tandem with two or more fuel dispensers in a single traffic lane. This arrangement can make it difficult for a customer to access a forward dispenser when the traffic lane is blocked by another customer.

franchise fee. An upfront fee charged to operators by the franchisor to license a concept.

fuel dispenser. The device that dispenses fuel into a vehicle.

fuel service. The improvements used in the dispensing and sale of retail motor fuel. Fuel service includes underground storage tanks (USTs), dispensers, canopies, electronics, and piping.

gallonage. An industry term that refers to the annual or monthly volume of fuel a store sells.

gondola. A merchandise display unit with shelves or pegs to display prepackaged products. Gondolas are usually premanufactured and generic in design.

gross fuel margin. The difference between what the wholesaler charges for a gallon of gasoline and the retail price the convenience store owner-operator can obtain in the local market.

hyper convenience store. A large convenience store with 4,000 to 5,000 square feet of space that offers an array of products and services arranged in various departments. A hyper convenience store may have a bakery, a sit-down restaurant, or a pharmacy and often sells gasoline. Such stores have many employees per shift, substantial parking spaces, and extended hours.

hypermarket. A retail property that combines a department store and a grocery store in one building.

in-store sales. Sales that are not fuel-related or produced as a result of a carwash business. In-store sales include merchandise, food service, and services and account for 40% to 50% of the typical convenience store's revenue.

intangible assets. Assets of a business that are not tangible real property or tangible personal property.

kiosk. A convenience store format of less than 800 square feet that is intended to provide additional revenue beyond gasoline sales. Gasoline is always the focus of this operation and the owner is usually an oil company or petroleum marketer. A kiosk sells only items found in traditional convenience stores such as tobacco, beverages, snacks, and confections.

labor costs. The largest category of annual operating expenses on the store owner's operating statement. Labor costs cover all employee compensation, including wages, payroll taxes, workers' compensation, health insurance, and other employee benefits.

limited selection convenience store. A store with 1,500 to 2,200 square feet of space that is often affiliated with an oil company. Both gasoline and store sales contribute to profitability, and simple food service such as hot dogs, nachos, or popcorn may be offered.

location quotient. A trade area analysis tool that can be adapted to a number of different uses. It measures the supply of and demand for convenience stores in a specific market and assumes that a broader geographic area, such as a state, reflects the same supply and demand relationship.

market saturation. Overbuilding in a particular market.

mechanical dispenser. An old type of fuel dispenser that is most easily identified by its analog display. The display shows the total purchase price and gallons of fuel dispensed. Mechanical dispensers cannot be easily adapted to pay-at-the-pump technology.

merchandise equipment. Personal property that includes all of the equipment and trade fixtures used in the display and sale of in-store items, i.e., shelving, free-standing coolers, freezers, and moveable counters.

mini convenience store. A store that has 800 to 1,200 square feet of space. Mini convenience stores are popular with oil companies because they focus on gasoline sales. Grocery selection is limited and there is no food service beyond prepared sandwiches. The only parking available is at the pumps.

mini-tunnel carwash. A type of exterior-only, automatic carwash that is shorter in length than most tunnel systems. The shorter length allows a mini-tunnel carwash to be installed on sites that are too small to accommodate conventional tunnel systems.

motor fuel device. A device designed to measure and deliver liquids used as fuel for internal-combustion engines.

multi-hose dispenser. A dispenser with one hose for each fuel type.

multiple-product dispenser (MPD). A dispenser with two, three, or four hoses from which several fuel grades can be selected.

multi-tier pricing. A system in which one type of fuel is sold at more than one price per gallon. The price depends on the delivery or payment method.

near corner. A corner located just before a traffic control device at an intersection. Along streets with high traffic volume, access to near corners is frequently blocked when traffic is stopped by vehicles waiting to pass through the intersection. Near corner sites are less desirable than far corner sites for convenience store locations.

pool margin. The average gross margin on all fuel products sold at a store during a period. Different grades of gasoline have different gross margins. Industry participants discuss pool margins rather than specific margins for different fuel grades.

product margin. The income remaining after the wholesale cost of the merchandise is paid.

proprietary database. A system that contains data on specialized property types and is used by real estate appraisers and analysts. Proprietary databases charge a fee for each property sale the user selects. Once selected, the sale information is transmitted via the Internet, a fax machine, or conventional mail. Sale properties may be identified by geographic area, property type, or both.

quick-service restaurant (QSR). A restaurant that offers a limited menu. Food is prepared quickly while the customer waits. Also called fast feeders and fast-food restaurants.

rack price. The wholesaler's cost of fuel, usually expressed in price per gallon. Convenience store operators frequently watch published rack prices to adjust retail prices at their stores. The rack price is the basis for changes in the wholesale cost of fuel.

remote dispenser system. A type of fuel delivery system in which a single pump at the storage tank supplies all of the dispensing units. If the pump fails, none of the dispensers will operate.

retail channel. Any specific category of stores in the retail industry. Convenience stores, drugstores, and fast-food restaurants are all examples of retail channels.

retail motor fuel device. A type of dispenser that is used for single fuel deliveries of less than 100 gallons, retail fuel deliveries to individual highway vehicles, and single deliveries of liquefied petroleum gas for domestic use and liquefied petroleum gas or liquid anhydrous ammonia for non-resale use.

ring study. A trade area analysis tool that divides the area surrounding the subject property into concentric zones, or rings. Ring studies analyze demographic and competitive characteristics. They do not recognize geographic barriers or traffic routes within the trade area.

royalties and advertising fees. Ongoing payments to the franchisor to cover administrative and marketing costs, usually based on a percentage of gross or net sales.

self-contained pump. A fuel delivery system in which each fuel dispenser includes an individual pump that pulls fuel from the storage tank. If one pump malfunctions, other dispensers can continue to operate.

self-service carwash. A non-automated carwash that uses wands and handheld brushes to dispense water, soap, and wax. The customer supplies the labor to wash and rinse the vehicle. These systems are usually coin-operated.

service station saturation index (SSSI). A trade area analysis tool developed by Texaco in the 1960s to assess the feasibility of constructing new service stations in specific locations.

shrink. Product loss caused by damage or the expiration of a product's freshness date.

spanner. An elevated concrete island where the fuel dispensers are located. Spanners help prevent the customer's vehicle from colliding with fuel dispensers.

starting gate design. A common fuel service layout in which fueling positions are arranged in a single row and each fuel dispenser has a separate traffic lane.

stock keeping unit (SKU). Each individual product sold in a convenience store.

store envelope. Area that includes the building footprint, the drive-thru lane, and parking.

supplies. An expense category that includes all purchases of items used in the management and operation of the business. These items are not for resale.

tangible assets. Business assets that can be classified as real property, personal property, or trade fixtures.

throughput. The number of cars that a carwash can accommodate per hour.

touchfree system. A carwash system in which no part of the washing equipment contacts the car, thus avoiding any scratches. A touchfree system often requires expensive chemicals, water heaters, and water softeners.

trade area. The geographic area within which the subject store competes for business.

trade dress. A feature added to a building, such as a sign or logo, which indicates that a convenience store is affiliated with a well-known brand.

traditional convenience store. A store with 2,400 to 2,500 square feet of space that offers a large product mix, including dairy, bakery, snacks, beverages, grocery, and more. Such operations are typically owned by convenience store chains.

underground storage tank (UST). A buried tank used to store motor fuel.

vapor lock. A condition created when fuel traveling from a cold storage tank through warmer pipelines vaporizes. Vapor lock typically occurs in improperly installed fuel dispensing systems and prevents fuel from reaching its destination.

wholesale motor fuel device. A dispenser used to deliver large quantities of fuel that will be resold.